I do not understand how anyone can live

without one small place of enchantment to turn to.

MARJORIE KINNAN RAWLINGS

ABOUT THE AUTHOR

Ellen Dugan, also known as the Garden Witch, is a psychic-clairvoyant who lives in Missouri with her husband and three teenage children. A practicing Witch for over eighteen years, Ellen also has many years of nursery and garden center experience, including landscape and garden design. She received her Master Gardener status through the University of Missouri and her local county extension office. Look for other articles by Ellen in Llewellyn's annual Magical Almanac, Wicca Almanac, and Herbal Almanac. Visit her website at:

www.geocities.com/edugan_gardenwitch

INCLUDES HOUSEHOLD JOURNAL

COTTAGE WITCHERY

❧ NATURAL MAGICK FOR HEARTH AND HOME ❧

ELLEN DUGAN

Llewellyn Publications
Saint Paul, Minnesota

FIRST EDITION
First Printing, 2005

Book design and editing by Rebecca Zins
Cover design by Lisa Novak
Cover image © Richard Cummins, Superstock
Interior illustrations © 2005 Kerigwen

Llewellyn is a registered trademark of Llewellyn Worldwide, Ltd.

Library of Congress Cataloging-in-Publication Data

Dugan, Ellen, 1963-
   Cottage witchery : natural magick for hearth and home / Ellen Dugan.—1st ed.
      p.   cm.
   Includes bibliographical references and index.
   ISBN 0-7387-0625-6
   1. Magic.   2. Home—Miscellanea.   3. Witchcraft.   I. Title.

BF1623.H67D84 2005
133.4'3—dc22

2004061536

Llewellyn Worldwide does not participate in, endorse, or have any authority or responsibility concerning private business transactions between our authors and the public.
   All mail addressed to the author is forwarded but the publisher cannot, unless specifically instructed by the author, give out an address or phone number.
   Any Internet references contained in this work are current at publication time, but the publisher cannot guarantee that a specific location will continue to be maintained. Please refer to the publisher's website for links to authors' websites and other sources.

Llewellyn Publications
A Division of Llewellyn Worldwide, Ltd.
P.O. Box 64383, Dept. 0-7387-0625-6
St. Paul, MN 55164-0383, U.S.A.
www.llewellyn.com

Printed in the United States of America

CONTENTS

Contents

CHAPTER FOUR

DEITIES, FAERIES, AND MAGICK OF THE HEARTH FLAME, 71

Contents

CHAPTER NINE
HAPPINESS AND HARMONY IN THE HOME, 199

Contents

ACKNOWLEDGMENTS

This book was written during a transitional period in my life. One of my kids graduated from high school and then went off to college. My second son hit his senior year of high school and started his own college preparations. My youngest turned sixteen and started learning how to drive. And if that wasn't enough excitement, I switched to a part-time job to focus more on my "second job"—writing—and I turned the big 4-0.

During all of the upheaval, excitement, challenge, and change in my life, a few friends stood by to encourage and support me. They listened, held my hand and, most importantly, made me laugh. A very special thank-you goes to Paula, Gwen, Colleen, Heather, Scott, Jennifer, and Nicole for all of the reasons listed above, and for so much more.

To my writing buddies Christopher and Dorothy, thanks for the camaraderie, the fun, the good advice and, most importantly, for your friendship.

To Natalie Harter, acquisitions editor extraordinaire, who was enthusiastic about the idea from the beginning. To Becky Zins, my editor, for letting me bounce ideas off of her and who is always a pleasure to work with. And to Megan Atwood, just because you're so much fun. Thanks to Kerigwen for the lovely artwork.

Finally, for my family, who keeps encouraging me. To my sons Kraig and Kyle, who are both growing up into such fine young men. To my witchy teenage daughter Kat (watch out, witching world, she's going to knock your striped socks off!). And last but not least, to my wonderful and loving husband of twenty-three years, Ken.

I love you all.

I knew by the smoke that so gracefully curl'd

Above the green elms that a cottage was near,

And I said, "If there is peace to be found in the world,

A heart that was humble might hope for it here."

THOMAS MOORE

THE MODERN WITCH'S COTTAGE

If you were to ask someone how to describe a Witch's house, they would probably describe a fictional and funky stone cottage set back along the edge of the woods. Perhaps they would visualize a gothic and grim mansion complete with fancy lattice ironwork and mysterious moss-draped trees. They would never imagine a cosmopolitan apartment or stylish condo, a rambling farmhouse, a simple duplex, a tidy two-story, or even a ranch-style house in the 'burbs. A Witch's home would have to be far outside of the average or mundane world, wouldn't it?

Well, yes and no. You can't spot a Witch's home by sight as much as you can identify it by sense. It's not the style or structure of the building that will tip you off. It's the feeling that resonates within you as you walk up to the front door. Witches, natural magicians, and other magick users typically make their homes

into sacred and protected places for themselves and for their family and pets. You can certainly look for magickal clues but they are much more subtle than most folks would imagine.

Perhaps there is a hex sign attached to the outside of the home. Is that a stone gargoyle making a hideous face at you while he guards the flower beds in the yard? Are there pots of deep red geraniums for protection on the porch arranged on either side of the front door? Look for window boxes or a hanging basket that spills over with magickal flowers and scented foliage, or silvery, celestial wind chimes that sing out on a breeze. These are enchanting clues to the natural magick that may be practiced within the home.

Expect that you will feel the tingle as you cross the threshold. As you enter, you discover a broom displayed bristle ends up, and an old horseshoe nailed open ends up over the inside front door. Perhaps there are a few clusters of crystals arranged in the living room to help keep the energy of the house and all those who live there on track. A few pots of fragrant green herbs are thriving in a sunny kitchen windowsill. A large iron cauldron perches on the hearth of the fireplace. Natural, seasonal decorations that change with the Sabbats are artfully displayed along a shelf or the mantel—perhaps at Lammas there is a bundle of wheat for fertility or golden-yellow candles to celebrate the first harvest. As the seasons progress, this may change into an arrangement of gourds or fall leaves at the autumnal equinox for abundance, and so on. Welcome to the simple enchantments and potent natural magick found in and around a Witch's home.

The Natural Magick of Hearth and Home

The natural magick of the home-based Witch is uncomplicated and down-to-earth. There is wisdom and spirituality evoked by the very earth that we live on. Why not take that basic energy and direct it into your home? Applying the subject of natural magick to your home is a great opportunity to get in touch with your sense of enchantment and to link back into the tides of nature to celebrate the cycles of the earth, the moon, and the seasons.

You may call yourself a cunning man, wise woman, hedge witch, kitchen witch, garden witch, or maybe you think of yourself as a natural magician. Perhaps you don't give yourself a title at all. A Witch's inner power comes from connecting to the influence and secrecy of the natural world that surrounds their home, family, and life. Natural magick is elemental, quiet, and spontaneous. I am a firm believer in the power and positive force of natural magick and the tradition of practicing a more down-to-earth and elemental-themed spirituality.

Working with the influences of nature to boost the power and security of our homes is not a new idea. Author Scott Cunningham described a magickal home as being a "pool of protective energy" and "a shrine to the deity of life itself." This is an elegant way of pointing out that your home is a sacred and influential magickal place. So now that you've wrapped your mind around this idea, what are you going to do about it? How can you apply this idea to your lifestyle in a natural and practical way?

If you are thinking *Well, I just live in a apartment, I don't have anything fancy,* let me point out that it's not about how much you spend or how fancy of a residence you live in—that matters not in the slightest. I am not expecting your home to look like a photo shoot for *Better Pagan Homes and Gardens.* Cottage witchery is about making magick with what you have, or can acquire affordably. Look at garage sales and flea markets for fun and charming decorative pieces. Watch for sales or make magickal and creative accessories yourself. Remember, natural and magickal décor and supplies do not have to be expensive. It is not about how much money you have or how big the place you call home is.

My mother is a pro at taking whatever she has on hand and turning it into something stunning. When I grew up, money was very tight and whatever seasonal decorations or furnishings we had was typically sewn, arranged, created, or reupholstered by my mom. I never appreciated how much her do-it-yourself style influenced both myself and my brother and sister until we were all grown and raising families of our own. That sense of welcome and practicality shows up in each of our homes, and that type of common sense is a magick unto itself.

The idea behind cottage witchery is to encourage folks to look at their homes in a new magickal way and to connect to a simpler time. No, I'm not asking you to give up your computers or to start washing your laundry on a rock down at the creek. I *am* encouraging you to reconnect to the energies of the natural world—to cherish, celebrate, and then to direct these magickal forces into your homes and everyday lives.

Go ahead and arrange a few sunflowers in an old glass canning jar and set it out on your table this summer. It will brighten up the whole room, just like magick. This autumn arrange a few mini pumpkins and gourds on a shelf and scatter a handful of oak leaves around them to celebrate wisdom and the earth's abundance during the harvest festivals.

How about setting a rustic basket of pine cones and pretty twigs that you gathered and arranged yourself on your hearth this winter? This would invoke an earthy type of enchantment, as the pine cones are symbols of fertility and the pine itself encourages prosperity. This is the essence of simple, affordable, and practical magick. Try looking at things from a natural magick perspective. Nature is beautiful. Imagine what fascinating energies you could incorporate into your life by bringing natural and rustic items into your home.

Cottage witchery is meant to inspire you to add a little old-time charm and down-to-earth magick into your everyday life.

This book is filled with witchy ideas, all of them no-nonsense and easy to incorporate into your magickal lifestyle. In *Garden Witchery* I took the reader outside into the garden to focus on how it affects your life and magick. This time I am bringing the reader inside, to encourage you to nest in and to create an enchanting and wonderful home where you can practice your natural witchcraft in a quiet and practical way. (You'll also learn a few tricks on how to create your own personalized spells and charms while we are at it.)

Together, we will explore deities for the hearth and home, and how to create some natural magick throughout your house. We'll whip up a little kitchen cupboard conjuring and explore fireplace magick. There will be ideas for celebrating the four seasons at home and magickal ideas for outdoor rooms. Finally we'll close up with three specialty chapters, each full of spells and charms that focus on creating protection, prosperity, and happiness for the home and family.

So, pull up a comfy chair and sit with me for a while. Enjoy the crackle of the logs in the wood-burning stove and have a cup of tea. Let's explore the idea of the thoroughly modern Witch's cottage and let's discuss magickal ideas for hearth and home. We'll weave a few elemental spells, conjure up some home-style enchantment, and give you lots of ideas on how to transform your abode into a place of comfort, contentment, and magick.

Cottage Witchery Charm

Whether apartment, condo, or house in the 'burbs,

Elements four gather 'round; Witches, hear these words;

For your homes are magickal places, as you will soon see,

Look to nature to provide the supplies that you will need.

Create happiness and harmony with simple, natural things;

Success, prosperity, and joy may this cottage witchery bring.

Chapter One

There is an emanation for the heart in genuine hospitality

which cannot be described but is immediately felt,

and puts the stranger at once at his ease.

WASHINGTON IRVING

A WITCHY WELCOME

Welcome and make yourself at home. Have a seat and let's you and I sit and chat. Hmm? What was that? Oh, thanks. We like our house too. I watch as your eyes dart around the living room, looking for signs of witchery. I smile to myself as, for the most part, the magickal accessories are pretty subtle. But I will admit there are a few things that jump right out at you.

Where did I get the stained glass pentacle, you ask? Oh, I made that years ago when I worked at a stained glass shop; everyone thought it was a hex sign. The big old cauldron sitting on the brick hearth? Found it for next to nothing at an antique shop, rusted and stuck in a corner. A little steel wool and black spray paint and it's as good as new.

Your eyes continue to search the room as the family's two cats come strolling in to check out the visitor. They may or may not grace you with their presence by sniffing you over and then perching behind you on the back of the sofa. Other than a few crystal clusters, to you everything looks pretty normal and lived in. Well, this isn't what you were expecting.

You rise and follow me into the kitchen at my question as to whether you'd like something to drink. As I pour your beverage into the glass, you look around the kitchen and check out the mossy-green painted walls and a crafty kitchen witch collection centered on a painted shelf.

The herb prints hanging on the walls draw you in for a closer look. Mounded on the counter is a variety of seasonal produce from our family's farm. I tell you to expect to take some home with you. There is way too much there for us to possibly eat.

We make our way back to the living room and you curl up comfortably on the couch, thinking to yourself that you are going to have to do a complete revamp of what you thought a real Witch's house would be. Hmm . . . so now that you are all snug on the couch, how do you feel? Safe, calm, happy, and at ease. Good, that's exactly how you should feel.

Disappointed at the lack of drama? Don't worry, I get that reaction a lot. I have had students come to my home for the first time expecting some suburban-type of Addam's family mansion. They were pretty uptight until they saw that we lived in a ranch-style home in the 'burbs. As they came in and sat on the couch I could see that they were scanning everything as fast as possible. When my three kids came flying down the hall engaged in hand to hand combat, they started to smile. When I excused myself to ask the kids . . . *okay,* to go and yell at the kids to knock it off, my guests started to laugh.

As I came back into the living room to join them, they were grinning. I could only smile back at them and say that what really makes a Witch's home different is the way that it makes you feel. The magickal home carries a particular type of positive psychic vibration. This type of enchanting energy is often expanded upon and refined by the Witch who dwells there. This sort of magickal emanation puts welcomed guests and family at ease. It is both a strength and a comfort. If you think about it, a home that exudes a sense of hospitality and welcome is a type of natural magick all of its own.

So you're here because you'd like to learn a few natural magick practices for your own hearth and home? Great, you've come to the right place! The tips and techniques of bringing a little witchery into the place where you live are both simple and down-to-earth. These are subtle types of magick: think handmade and homegrown—a leaf from a tree, a flower grown in the yard, herbs and spices, candle spells and color magick. The enchanting household accessories, charms, and spells may not be glaringly obvious to the casual observer, but they are powerful magick nonetheless. Many of the ingredients cottage witchery calls for are, more often than not, already readily available to you, possibly lurking about in the spice rack or outside, compliments of good old Mother Nature.

Now before you think to yourself *Oh, she's just going to talk about kitchen witch stuff,* let me point out a few things to you here. For starters, I really hate to cook. I *can* cook, I just would prefer not to. So don't worry, I will not be bombarding you with recipes. I'll leave that to the culinary magicians. Also, something else you may want to consider is that traditionally much of the spellwork of the wise women/cunning men originated from the hearth. And the hearth is where the family of olden times prepared herbal remedies, cooked their food, and gathered together. It was the natural place for magick, as the hearth exuded light and warmth and was literally the heart of the home.

Where we love is home,
home that our feet may leave,
but not our hearts.

OLIVER WENDELL HOLMES

THE MAGICKAL HEART OF THE HOME

Alas, today very few homes have a central hearth. They may lay claim to a fireplace or a wood-burning stove if they are fortunate, but for today's modern Witch the hearth area is actually the kitchen. Think about it. Dinner is prepared there, kids do their homework at the kitchen table, bills are paid, crises are faced, and games are played as the family gathers around the table. Whenever there is a gathering of family and friends, folks usually hang out in the kitchen. At circle meetings at my house, the ladies usually all end up crammed into the kitchen, laughing and snacking. My first thought was because that's where the food was, but nope, they always seem to congregate in the kitchen.

Where do you suppose the heart of your magickal home lies? Is it in the kitchen? Or is it in the living room, gathered around the coffee table, eating pizza with your kids and watching a movie? Is your favorite spot in a chair next to your fireplace? Or is it sitting out on your deck or back porch? Everyone's heart of the home will be unique, and that's as it should be. So while you're thinking about this, get up and take a walk around your place. Close your eyes after you enter the rooms and cast out your senses. Really try to get an impression for what type of energy you have going on in there. Typically you will find a couple of places that pull both visitors and family members alike.

Home is where the heart is, they say. And keep in mind that the most powerful magick always comes from the heart. That makes a modern Witch's home a powerful magickal place, to be sure. There is actually a spiritual connection between ourselves and our homes. When the energies of nature are welcomed within and our homes are blessed with magickal purpose, they do become sacred spaces. Within your magickal sanctuary, you'll always feel a bit of serenity, no matter where you live, how rotten your day at work was, or how much your kids drive you crazy.

If you want to start turning your place into a magickal sanctuary, you can begin by cleaning house. Think of this as cleaning not only on the physical level but also on the astral plane. The astral level is where magick lives. The astral can't always be seen but it can, with practice, be sensed. So we should not overlook this important aspect while we prepare to clean house. If you approach this task with magickal intention, then it becomes an act of magick. Let's send those dust bunnies and old negativity on their way! Haul out the vacuum and the broom, and get out the dust rag. Visualize that you are capturing old hurt feelings and unpleasant emotions while you sweep. As you dust and polish, imagine that you are wiping away grime and bad luck. Here's a cottage witchery tip: If you use a lemon-scented furniture polish, the scent of lemons will help dispel bad vibes and negativity. How about those curtains—when was the last time they were washed? What about the shades or blinds, could they stand to be wiped down? Add a drop or two of lavender oil to your cleaning water and cleanse those blinds or shades while you freshen things up.

Clean your house from top to bottom, get rid of the clutter, and then take out the garbage. Take a hard look at what's lying around and see what you can dispose of. Toss out old magazines, recycle the old newspapers and aluminum cans, donate old clothes or kid's outgrown ones to a shelter, and clear all of that extra junk out of your home. Try burning a little incense while you clean. Sandalwood's a good choice—typically this scent is used to promote spirituality and to remove negativity. Or—weather permitting—open the windows and let the fresh air in.

Finally, go take a look at your magickal bookshelf or cabinet. Could it stand to be reorganized and straightened out as well? Yup, I thought so. Mine always manages to become untidy too. I don't know how it happens, but I always seem to be straightening it back up. How it manages to get so messy in the first place is a constant mystery to me.

Once you've gotten the clutter and the mess under control, we can begin to work our cottage witchery. By taking control of your surroundings you can begin to trigger the natural magick of your hearth and home. Those elemental energies are all around you anyway, why not direct them toward creating harmony in your life? Now that your place is clean and sparkling on both the physical and astral planes, we are ready to begin. Where do we start, you may wonder? We start by blessing the heart of your home.

A NATURAL MAGICK BLESSING
FOR THE HEART OF THE HOME

Here is a natural magick blessing to try out. Why am I diving into this so quickly? Because I am a hands-on type of Witch. I want to give you some magick to perform right away. You are going to be very busy for a while getting your magickal home in order . . . so, let's get to it! Pick the room or rooms that you feel are the heart of your home and gather these simple and elemental supplies.

* A small dish of salt to represent the earth and prosperity

* A stick of incense (your choice of scent) and a holder; the scented smoke represents air and knowledge

* A red candle and a coordinating candleholder for fire and courage

* A small bowl of water for water and love

* Matches or a lighter

Straighten and clean the room or rooms to be blessed. Then light the candle and the incense. Place the candle in the center of the room. Beginning in the east, and moving in a deosil (clockwise) motion, work your way slowly around the room. First sprinkle a bit of salt in each corner. Then carry the incense around, waving a little of the smoke to help it flow. Next sprinkle a bit of the water around the perimeter of the room. Then settle in front of the candle and visualize the blessings from each of the four elements.

There is the gift of prosperity from deep in the earth. Knowledge is sent along a fragrant breeze from the air. Courage is rewarded to you from the bright, dancing flames of fire, and love embraces you from the emotional element of water. Picture these elemental gifts in your mind and then visualize both you and the people or pets who live with you receiving an equal share of these offerings. When you are ready, center yourself and repeat this blessing:

Elements four I call, release now your power,

As I bless my home in this magickal hour.

No negativity can enter, no spirits shall roam,

As I consecrate and protect the heart of my home.

As you finish the charm, draw a circle in the air above the candle flame with your finger. Spiral it up faster and faster, higher and higher, until you fling the energy off and out into the room. Then close up the spell by saying,

This home is now blessed by my will and desire,

I close this spell by earth, air, water, and fire.

You may allow the candle and the incense to burn themselves out. Afterward make sure to tidy up all of your supplies. Does the house feel better? I bet if you pay attention, you'll notice a subtle change in people's reactions as they enter the heart of your home. Now that your home is on track and has a nice magickal sparkle, it will radiate out to the rest of the place. So, are you ready to learn more? I figured you would be. Let's start by taking a look at some other equally enchanting household areas. A few of these you may have never even thought of, such as the opening or threshold of your home.

Bewitched is half of everything.

NELLY SACHS

ENCHANTED ENTRANCES
AND BEWITCHED BACKDOORS

Doorways are in between places. Therefore they are considered to be magickal. So why not take a look at this idea from a witchy perspective and see what we can conjure up? It's time to concentrate on the entrances to your enchanting home.

First impressions are absolutely important. The threshold of the Witch's home sets a tone and introduces a sort of ambiance. Visitors to your place will probably feel it as they step up to the door. This can be a feeling of welcome to friends and family or it could be a feeling of warning or unease to intruders. If you are going through the trouble of creating a home that sparkles with magickal energy, why not set the mood right off the bat?

There is the old, enchanting tradition of painting your front door blue. The color blue is both a magickal and peaceful color. It represents the element of water, healing, and protection. A blue door also denotes a magickal safe house. White-painted window frames and sashes were believed to keep out unwanted influences as well. And speaking of windows, if you have a front or back door that has a window in it, then try adding a stained glass panel to your door's window. A few celestial-style patterns, Pennsylvania Dutch hex sign patterns, or something more art nouveau can be a very magickal addition indeed.

If stained glass is out of your budget, then take a look at the arts and crafts stores for stick-on strips of leading and glass paints and patterns. This is a great way to get the look of stained glass and it's easy to do. These glass paints and leading strips can give an average door window a magickal, stained glass look at a fraction of the cost. Plus it's a good excuse to be magickally creative all at the same time. What sort of design would you add to your front door? Elemental symbols, stars, floral patterns? The sky's the limit.

How about adding bewitching plants in containers to your front porch? Try red geraniums for protection or pink geraniums to promote love. An ivy growing along the house is protective and a honeysuckle vine promotes prosperity. Hang up window boxes and stuff them full of aromatic and magickal herbs, colorful flowers, and foliage. Consider planting begonias in your window boxes. These shade- and sun-loving annuals symbolize a protective warning.

I plant begonias in my window boxes every year for protection and because they perform beautifully in the part-sun, part-shade area of my back patio. Also, according to local Midwestern folklore, the way to spot the "good Witches" in the neighborhood was by the red geraniums or red begonias growing in window boxes at their homes.

Witchy Wreaths, Garlands, and Accessories

Here is a subtle magickal idea: try hanging up a seasonal wreath and blessing it for prosperity and protection. It will be the first thing visitors see as they walk up to your door, so make it a magickal greeting. You could be really elaborate and have a separate wreath for each Sabbat or you could make a wreath for each season. Or take one grapevine wreath and simply tuck in seasonal silk flowers and sprigs of dried herbs and switch them out at the season's change. Wreaths, whether they are simple or complex, are full of magick, texture, and beauty. They are wonderful symbols for a magickal welcome. I dare you to go to the arts and crafts store and see what you could create for your own place. Glue guns are cheap; imagination is priceless.

Here is another intriguing suggestion. Arrange a set of lights along with seasonal greenery around the outside of your front door. Not just for Yuletide, decorative garlands may be used around your door at any season. Just imagine what you could do with those! Sure, pine garlands are traditional at the winter holidays, but use your imagination for the other seasons as well. I do recommend using silk foliage and accessories as this will be outdoors and exposed to the elements. (It will also last for a few seasons as opposed to a week or two if it's fresh.)

For the fall, consider adding a garland of artificial autumn-colored leaves with tiny orange lights for Mabon through Samhain. Tuck in some apples or gourds to the fall display. During the spring months, use ivy intertwined with white fairy lights and springtime flowers. In the summer, how about a garland of red roses or bright sunflowers with those tiny lights? You could tuck little grapevine stars into the garland or whatever other witchy things you can conjure up. This way you are celebrating the seasons and the Sabbats and you can be as discreet or flamboyant as you wish.

WARDING YOUR DOORWAYS

Doorways can easily be warded to keep intruders or negativity out. When you ward doorways, it's like setting up a magickal alarm system. If anyone or thing tries to enter that wasn't invited or doesn't belong, the wards above the doorways are supposed to give the owner of the home a little "tweak." This can be as subtle as a vague discomfort or pulling sensation at your solar plexus, or it may be an all-out adrenaline rush of warning, not to mention the uncomfortable effect it has on the unwanted "guest" who enters un-invited. Interested? Here are a few quick ideas for wards that you can make yourself and then add over the doorways of your home.

Create a swag out of dried flowers and herbs to create a magickal archway over the inside of your door. In many craft stores they have basic unadorned eucalyptus swags and lots of dried flowers available for arranging. Eucalyptus is a good base to start with, as it symbolizes health and protection. Now roll up your sleeves, break out the glue gun, and prepare to get creatively witchy with this basic swag.

Here is a list of common dried magickal flowers often found at the arts and crafts store. Take a look at this Witch's dozen of dried supplies and see what you would like to incorporate into this warding swag for your doorway. Note that you may refer to this list when scouting out herbal supplies for your witchy wreaths and garlands as well.

AMARANTH/GLOBE FLOWER: protection

BABY'S BREATH: a pure heart and happiness

FEVERFEW: health and protection

LUNARIA (HONESTY): money and repels monsters, according to folklore

LAVENDER: dispels bad luck and is protective; smells wonderful too!

LARKSPUR: friends are welcome

LOTUS PODS: good luck and blessings

ROSES: love

THISTLE: protection

SUNFLOWERS: loyalty and admiration

QUEEN ANNE'S LACE: safe house and return home

WHEAT: fertility and prosperity

YARROW: all-purpose, the wise woman's herb

Don't be afraid to add ribbons to coordinate with your room or to employ a bit of color magick. Once you have finished with your swag, you'll need to enchant it for protection and then put it up in place to create your ward. Try repeating this warding charm as you prepare to attach the swag over the inside of the main entrance to your home.

Magickal herbs, flowers, and ribbons make up this warding spell,

Alert me to danger and protect my home that's loved so well.

By the magick of plants, I ask to be given a "tweak,"

May this warding spell hold true, day to day and week to week.

Attach the swag over your door. Straighten and adjust as necessary. Close the warding charm up by saying:

For the good of all, with harm to none,

By flower and leaf, this spell is done!

But Wait . . . There's More!

Here are a few more simple, easy, and earthy ideas. Scattering various herbs such as dried and crumbled betony (otherwise known to gardeners as perennial lamb's ears) across the threshold is thought to keep all negative influences out of the home. Sprinkling a bit of salt on the windowsills was thought to have the same effect. One old Ozark folk magick trick to keeping the front door warded was to place holey stones under the steps or the front porch. Look for holed stones whenever you are out and about in nature. My family and I typically find them in and around streams or creek beds. Any rock with a naturally occurring hole in it is a holey stone. Perhaps you can tuck a few of those holey stones into your window boxes or hanging baskets that adorn your front porch. Then you have the bonus of the protective stones plus the magickal energies of the plants working together.

As mentioned in the introduction, a horseshoe nailed upright over the inside doorway was thought to bring good luck and prosperity to the family. This popular lucky charm was always supposed to be displayed with the open ends pointing up—that way your luck will never run out. The only time a horseshoe is to be displayed ends down is over a blacksmith's forge. Then it is thought that all of the good luck is spilled out onto the forge. Where to find an old horseshoe? Try the flea market. I bought one years ago for just a few bucks.

Horseshoes are thought to mimic the curves of the crescent moon so this could also be used as a moon-goddess symbol for your home. As you hang your horseshoe up and over the door, try this little charm to go along with it.

By the gods of old—Diana, Pan, and Puck,
May this horseshoe bring our home tons of good luck!

Hex Signs for the Threshold

Here is a popular spin on an old American brand of folk magick, the hex sign. Have you ever considered displaying a hex sign by your door? On the front of my house there are two hex signs. One is large and in the center of the front of the house; we made that one ourselves. It features a five-pointed star with a heart in the center. On the porch, next to the mailbox, is a smaller one that we purchased at an arts and crafts festival. This smaller hex sign spells out "welcome" in German and has two distelfink birds intertwined with flowers and stars. Since our families have German heritage, we thought this would be a fun addition to our porch. Now, if you are wondering if you can only display hex signs on the outside of the home, the answer is no. This type of folk art is subtle and very magickal, and you can display one wherever you wish. I even have one hanging in my kitchen to encourage prosperity.

Hex signs are symbols intended to bestow good luck, wealth, or protection. These striking geometric designs were produced with the belief that they would ward off bad luck and preserve peace, love, and prosperity in the home. Families chose their hex signs based on the colors, design, and the meaning. Some popular symbols included:

TULIP: faith

STARS: five points represent protection and good luck; eight points represent the wheel of the year

HEARTS: love

A DISTELFINK (a stylized representation of the goldfinch): good luck and good fortune

THE DOUBLE ROSETTE OR SIX-POINTED STAR: for protection; this was especially well liked. This "star" actually looks more like an open flower and is sometimes referred to as a *hexefus*.

According to my teenage kids, who are all taking German in school, this word means "witch's foot." Another fun bit of folk magick trivia is the German word for six, *sechs*, sounds like hex, and it is thought that this is how the hex sign got its name.

It's believed the hex sign originated in Europe. It has been used for protection and decoration on barns and in homes as folk art. This type of artwork was also featured on early furniture and family papers in America. When my mother-in-law gave us a copy of my husband's ancestors' papers, who had emmigrated from Germany, the family register was illustrated with six-pointed rosette-stars surrounded by circles—in other words, hex signs.

Hex signs have really become popular as a decorative item in the last few decades. There are dozens of magickal patterns and colors to choose from. The colors also play an important role in the sign. Red is for intense emotions, passion, and strength. White is for purity and is the typical background color. Yellow is for creativity and the sun. Blue is for protection, and green is for prosperity. Black is for defense and to tie all of the magick together.

Popular designs include a welcome with the two distelfinks and various pointed stars and scallops, all with separate magickal meanings. Interestingly enough, hex signs were historically thought to have warded off Witches. It's sort of ironic that many Witches today enjoy having hex signs to decorate their homes with. Sometimes magick is where you least expect it.

That's the thing about magic;
you've got to know it's still here, all around us,
or it just stays invisible for you.

CHARLES DE LINT

A Magickal Cottage All Your Own

No matter where you live, in the city or a rural area, cottage witchery can successfully be employed to create a little enchantment in your home. But you need to be creative. For example, if you can't decorate the outside of your door, then common sense tells us to work around the inside of the doors. Are you worried that a wreath or hex sign may be stolen from your apartment's front door? Well, then, hang it on the inside! Many apartments have a deck, patio area, or even a little fire escape. Set a few pots of flowers or herbs out there; see what you can conjure up. How about a few houseplants on the windowsill? Use your imagination! Don't be afraid to take the material that is presented here and adapt it to make it uniquely your own.

Cottage witchery is about finding modern and charming ways to creatively turn the place where you live into one of comfort, happiness, beauty, and magick. Cottage witchery embraces a magickal style and atmosphere in the home that is happy, humble, and definitely hands-on. It isn't about little wood sprites that dance merrily around a cottage, snuggled into an enchanted forest.

This is real life. You *can* turn your dreams into reality, right now and wherever you happen to live. Go ahead, turn the page and let's add a few more touches of whimsical enchantment into your life and into your home.

Chapter Two

Home is a name, a word, it is a strong one;

stronger than magician ever spoke,

or spirit ever answered to,

in the strongest conjuration.

CHARLES DICKENS

NATURAL MAGICK ALL AROUND THE HOME

We've begun our cottage witchery by focusing on the heart of the magickal home and by concentrating on the enchanting entrances to your residences. Now that we are on a roll, let's take a look at how to incorporate natural magick all around the house.

BRINGING THE OUTDOORS IN

The quickest way to add a bit of natural magick to your place is by bringing the outdoors in and decorating your magickal home with the warmth, beauty, and simplicity of nature. By using nature as our inspiration, we can soften the boundaries between the indoors and outdoors. You can start the transformation by adding greenery: plants in all shapes and sizes. Live plants add a healthy energy and vibration to the magickal home. Pick out something easy to care for and set the plant in a nice sunny spot. (There will be more information on magickal houseplants in chapter 6.)

To further introduce the four elements, maybe you could gather some fresh herbs like lavender, rosemary, or sage together and hang them up to dry. Their herbal aromas would invoke the element of air. What about one of those little fountain kits? The sound of running water would be great for encouraging relaxation, and you would be bringing the element of water into your house or apartment. For the element of earth, display some pretty, smooth pebbles in a wooden or ceramic bowl. If you added a few creamy-colored candles to this arrangement, you'd have all the representations of the elements on hand and in your room, ready to work magick with.

Incorporating cottage witchery into your home's décor means that you look for accent pieces that signify something special to you. Forget a slick, expensive, or modern look. And don't let yourself become overwhelmed at the thought of magickal redecorating. This is not a reality decorating show and you do have more than forty-eight hours in which to transform your home. So relax and enjoy yourself. When brainstorming for possible ideas, think of objects valued for their magickal or emotional appeal instead of how much cash you'll have to spend.

Check garage sales and flea markets. I once found a great old watering can at a flea market. I paid much less for it than I would have at an antique shop. It looks great in the living room next to the wood-burning stove. Rummage through your parents' or grandparents' attics and sheds. What time-worn pieces can you find that add a little history or subtle magick to your place?

For example, in my living room there is a large and worn antique picket fence gate hanging on the wall. Now, I will confess that I had seen this "look" in a slick gardening magazine and thought it would look great in our house, but I had no idea where I could affordably find one. I had the idea that not only would it bring a garden style into the living room but I could also enchant the gate for protection.

When I showed the magazine photo to my husband, he agreed with me that it would be a great accent piece for the room. Then he got very quiet and stared off into the distance, which frustrated me as I figured he probably wasn't paying any attention to a word I had just said.

"Got an idea," he announced. He dropped a distracted kiss on the top of my head and told me that he'd be back later. He was out the door like a shot and I could only sit and wonder what in the world had gotten into him. About an hour later he pulled up in the driveway and called one of our teenage sons to help him unload something out of the back of the truck. Curious, I wandered outside to discover a sturdy picket fence gate. The white paint was peeling in places. It was more than a little dirty and was covered in spider webs. But underneath the grime, it had the worn look I had been dreaming of.

"Where did you find that?" I asked him.

He informed me that it had been hanging in his grandmother's shed for years, gathering dust. He checked with his folks and they didn't mind if he took it—actually I think they thought he was a little strange wanting an old, dirty gate. But one man's trash is another man's treasure. So we carried our "treasure" into the backyard, sprayed it off with a hose, and sent those spiders scrambling into the garden. Then we took a wire brush to the wood to remove any flaking paint.

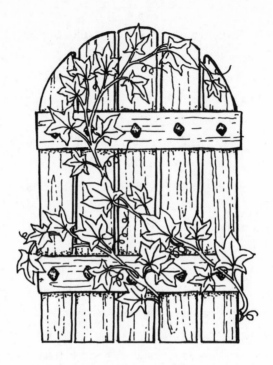

Ends up the gate was built by my husband's late grandfather for his wife many years ago. We estimated the gate to be around eighty years old. Once the gate was dry, my husband made a few minor repairs and we mounted it to the living room wall. His family was amazed at how well it cleaned up. In truth, it worked out really well for everyone. I got my gate to add to the garden theme and to enchant for our family's protection, and he acquired a wonderful memento of his grandparents.

The whole thrill of junking is that
you just know the next table will have
what you've been looking for all your life.

MARY RANDOLPH CARTER

FROM MUNDANE TO MAGICKAL

If you have that "scavenger gene" and like to hunt for bargains, check out tag sales, garage sales, and local flea markets. Try a few antique stores. Check with friends and relatives, see if they have any older pieces that they want to get rid of or sell. An old sideboard or rustic table would make a great altar. How about an ornamental wooden shelf for a wall altar? Come on, use your imagination! Once you've found your treasure, take it home and, if necessary, clean it up. Then enchant the piece for good luck or to bring protection.

A PROTECTION CHARM TO SHUT OUT NEGATIVITY

Here is the protection charm that I used for our antique gate.

Covered in grime and dust, I now make you brand new,
I enchant you with protection, my need is true.
By the powers of earth, air, fire, and water,
Shut out all harm, and keep in love and laughter.

Don't be afraid to adapt this charm to suit what treasure you have found. Remember the salvaged cauldron that I mentioned in the opening of the first chapter? It was old and rusted when I found it, but it was still sound. A little steel wool, elbow grease, and a can of black rust-proof spray paint and it was as good as new. You could adapt the following charm to consecrate furniture, a shelf, or to empower an old cauldron made new for magickal purposes. Take a look at the opening line of this next charm and change it to suit the item.

A TRANSFORMATION CHARM

Place your hands on the revamped item. Picture the four natural elements of earth, air, fire, and water swirling around you in a multicolored ring and into the piece. Then repeat this charm three times:

> *Forgotten and dusty/rusted, I now make you brand-new.*
> *Transform from mundane to magick, my need is true.*
> *By the powers of earth, air, fire, and water,*
> *I will conjure up love, good luck, health, and laughter.*

If you wish, you may add this closing line:

> *By the powers of earth and sea,*
> *As I will it, so must it be.*

What do you have laying around your place that could be transformed into a new magickal accessory? I bet that if you dig around, you'll find something that you could personalize or freshen up. Sometimes all it takes is a fresh perspective to add a touch of enchantment into your life.

With color one obtains an energy

that seems to stem from witchcraft.

HENRI MATISSE

COLORFUL IDEAS FOR ADDING
MAGICK TO YOUR HOME

Any Witch worth their broomstick knows about the power and possibilities of color magick. The fastest way to add magick all around the home is with the clever use of color. It's also the most striking and inexpensive way to change the feel of a room. Try breaking out a can of paint. Take a trip to the fabric store and choose an enchanting pattern and hue to add a little pizzazz into your rooms. Whip up some new pillows or fan out a pretty throw or afghan. Change the color of your bed linens or sew up a new duvet cover.

Freshening up your rooms with color can turn a bland, ordinary room into one with magickal personality and charm. Get inspired by a favorite print or poster on which you could base your color scheme. Neutrals are all the rage right now, and there is something to be said for introducing some natural and earthy tones into your home. Color trends may come and go, but trust your instincts.

Start with your favorite color and see where this leads you. For example, if you love green today, odds are that you'll still enjoy it years from now. If you like softer colors, then keep your shades softer and more pastel—if you have a thing for green, then you'd be looking at mint or a quiet apple green. If you like deep and dramatic tones and shades, then go for a richer, more vibrant tone of green, such as mossy green or even a forest green.

Most importantly, remember to follow your heart and your own taste. What colors are you drawn to? Which ones soothe or excite? What colors seem to complement your personality? This will give you plenty to think about for a while. And we can really take this bright idea a step further and take a look at your astrological signs and their coordinating elemental colors, because color magick isn't just for candles, you know.

THE ELEMENTS, ASTROLOGY, AND COLOR

Take, for example, whether you are an earth sign such as a Virgo, Capricorn, or Taurus. These folks are practical and down-to-earth, organized and sensual. Earth signs love material comforts: soft, lived-in fabrics, lots of different textures, and earthy colors. Natural looking wood finishes, hardwood floors, and the texture of brickwork or stone. The deep, earthy tones of brown, bronze, copper, and green will suit you right down to the ground and help you feel that connection to nature that you crave.

If your astrological sign is a watery one such as Cancer, Scorpio, or Pisces, then you are a sensitive soul. Water signs are emotional, intuitive, and easily influenced by their home environment. Try creating calm and peaceful rooms with the oceanic shades of blue and sea greens, purple and indigo. These watery tones ought to alleviate stress and lift your spirits. Add bleached out or pale, whitewashed furniture and fill up a pretty glass bowl with seashells. Add a small aquarium and bring some colorful fish into the room.

If you are a feisty, fiery sign of Aries, Leo, or Sagittarius, you are enthusiastic and more willing to be bold and daring with your personal space. Fire signs like spontaneity and are passionate and romantic. With a fire sign, anything from medieval to modern could work. Perhaps you enjoy bright red and white quilts and a more country look, or a lipstick-red sofa or crimson bedspread with black lacquered furniture—even antiques, dark woods, and heavy, opulent burgundy fabrics. Fire signs could be into any or all of these. They may rearrange things and try out new looks quite often. Tones of burgundy, red, and terra cotta; warm shades of orange and gold together with accents of dark woods or even bright white will add the drama and excitement you crave. Plus it will spice your home's décor right up.

If you fall under the influence of the element of air and are a Gemini, Libra, or Aquarius, you are prone to being intellectual, objective, and very communicative. Try a more modern or minimalist look. Pare down clutter and streamline your rooms. Add clear or frosted glass and mirrors to reflect light and to visually open up the room. Think of bright and airy open spaces that let the light and the air flow through. Then look to yellows (from buttery soft to bright), quiet neutrals, pastels, creams, and the very palest of blues.

Now, if you have taken a look at this astrological color information and wrinkle your nose up at your suggested colors (and sometimes that does happen), then consider checking out the following handy-dandy color list. As mentioned before, blue could cover any shade, from pale baby blue to denim to navy. The basic correspondence stays pretty much the same for the color, no matter what shade it happens to be. Use your imagination, try looking at this from a witchy perspective, and see what you can conjure up for your place.

Nature always wears the colors of the spirit.

RALPH WALDO EMERSON

A COLORFUL NATURAL MAGICK CORRESPONDENCE CHART

BLACK: removes negativity, is powerful, and establishes boundaries (which is probably why my teenage daughter has black curtains and a black bedspread in her bedroom)

BLUE: the element of water; peaceful, healing, and soothing

BROWN: earthy, stable, grounding, and comforting

COPPER: earthy and rich; a lucky color that is thought to encourage healing and prosperity

GOLD: opulence, wealth, the sun; a god color

GREEN: the element of earth; prosperous, stable; a Faerie Kingdom color

GREY/NEUTRAL: neutral, soothing; a harmonious color for homes

IVORY: sentimental feelings, memories, and coziness

ORANGE: energizing, exciting, warm; a harvest color

PINK: a "warm fuzzy" color; soothing, quietly romantic, and relaxing

PURPLE: magickal, spiritual, passionate, powerful

RED: the element of fire; lustful, vital, loving, and warm

SILVER: mystique, illusion, the moon, and a goddess color

WHITE: all-purpose, the moon, fresh, pure; a great basic starting point

YELLOW: the element of air, spring; creative and knowledgeable

These colors and their magickal associations should give you a starting point. Remember that colors can always be changed by softening or brightening up their tones and by adding complementary colors to go along with your home's décor. Experimenting with the use of color magick in your home is a very individualized process and it takes a bit of instinct, trial and error and, most of all, practice. But it is fun trying out those new magickal ideas and the possibilities are endless. Add a few touches of color into your rooms and see what sort of transformation you can achieve.

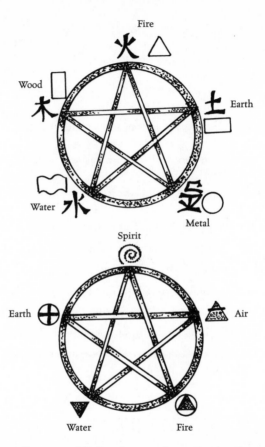

This is a great illustration of the five elements of Feng Shui (no, I'm not reinventing the pentagram). The Chinese elements are at the top and the traditional Wiccan elemental symbols are at the bottom. See pages 44 and 45 for elemental charms to coordinate with these illustrations.

By the transformation of yang

and its union with yin, the five agents arise:

water, fire, wood, metal, and earth.

CHOU TUN-YI

HEY, WHAT ABOUT FENG SHUI?

Feng Shui literally means "wind and water," and it is the 5,000-year-old art of arranging and decorating your home to encourage a happy life, well-being, prosperity, and contentment. The basic idea of Feng Shui is that everything in your surroundings, including the furnishings and color of your home, can either influence your life in a positive way or hinder your success. Feng Shui bases its principles of balance and harmony on the concepts of ying and yang (masculine and feminine), the five elements, and the eight directions. Feng Shui also encourages the use of positive *chi* or energy. With Feng Shui, you direct how energy flows through your rooms and your house.

Using the five elements of Feng Shui in your magickal home is a fascinating concept. Most magickal users will notice a bit of a difference between the Wiccan traditional elements of earth, air, fire, water, and spirit and the following ones listed here. In Feng Shui the five elements are represented as water, wood (sometimes called "tree"), fire, earth (occasionally referred to as "soil"), and metal. The ability to manipulate chi by using the five elements is the basis of many Feng Shui decorating remedies and designs. Try adding a touch of all the Feng Shui elements into your life and home, and see what changes you can bring about.

THE FIVE ELEMENTS OF FENG SHUI

WOOD shapes are rectangular and tall, thin, and vertical. Wood's season is spring and color is green. Folks who feel a strong connection to this Feng Shui element are outgoing, full of life, artistic, and hard working. Materials to incorporate are wood, wicker, bamboo, and paper. The element of wood corresponds with the east. The associations that go with the element of wood—some texts call this element "tree"—are just as you'd imagine, these being life, expansion, energy, and movement.

FIRE shapes are pointed, triangular, pyramid, zigzag, and star shaped. The season is midsummer, and the color is red. People who are attuned to this Feng Shui element are natural leaders that often inspire others to follow. They are passionate groundbreakers with a great sense of humor. Fire belongs to the south. Materials to work with include red flowers and pointed objects, crimson-colored, star-shaped candleholders, and red fabrics. The meanings of this element include passion, enthusiasm, warmth, and communication.

EARTH shapes are low, squat, flat, wide, and horizontal. The season is early fall, the colors are yellow and brown. Earth people are practical and loyal to their friends. These folks are the proverbial rock in a stressful situation and a pillar of strength in a crisis. This element corresponds with the north. The associated materials include plaster, china, ceramics, bricks, and natural fibers such as cotton, linen, wool, and silk. The elemental associations of earth or soil are comfort, security, prudence, and reliability.

METAL shapes are rounded and arched: domes, ovals, circles, and spheres. The season is late autumn and the corresponding colors are white, silver, and gold. Metal people are independent, determined, and can be single-minded. They are, however, extremely organized souls who prefer everything to be in its proper place. The element of metal corresponds to the west. Materials to incorporate include stainless steel, brass, silver, bronze, copper, iron, and gold. The meanings of this element are wealth, strength, leadership, and orderliness.

WATER shapes are irregular and wavy, curved and fluid. The season is midwinter, the color is black, and the recommended material is glass. Water people are great communicators, persuasive, and very sensitive to the feelings of others. Natural diplomats, they are excellent negotiators. This element is also aligned with the north. The magickal associations of this final element are depth, power, flexibility, peace, and tranquility.

These Feng Shui effects will be especially powerful if you combine the colors with the particular patterns or materials. One book suggests green vertical-striped wallpaper to represent earth/tree energy. A tall green lamp, a small pot of lucky bamboo, and green upright plants would do the same.

For fire, use red candles or clear, decorative oil lamps with red liquid paraffin inside; star-shaped votive holders in metallic red (bet you'll find those around the winter holiday season); fresh red flowers, like carnations and roses; and red luxurious fabrics and pillows.

To bring the chi of earth/soil into your home, try adding a window-box type of terra-cotta container. The shape, color, and the potting soil within pretty much cover all the bases. See if you can add a low-growing houseplant with yellow on the foliage or yellow-colored flowers, or add to your home's décor a square yellow-gold frame or checkered fabrics in brown to golden yellow.

For metal, work with metal itself and round silver, gold, or white objects, like a circular-shaped, silver-edged mirror, a small silver gazing globe, rounded metallic wire sculptures, or a round metal planter or pot. How about round silver trinket boxes?

To introduce the chi of water, try introducing glass objects, small irregular-shaped dishes, or black fabrics on your upholstery that feature a flowing pattern. What about some of those shiny black glass marbles that are so popular nowadays? You could arrange those in a funky clear shallow dish for instant water energy. Wouldn't that be cool? Here are a few more nifty tips and tricks for adding a bit of Feng Shui chi to your home.

CRYSTALS: To add more positive chi to your home, try hanging crystal sun catchers in a sunny window. For Feng Shui purposes it is recommended to use the round, multifaceted crystal sun catchers. (The irregular-shaped sun catchers may cause spiky or unbalanced chi.) When the sunlight catches the globes, it refracts into rainbows, and then positive energy radiates out in all directions, pushing old, stagnant energy out and bringing in fresh energy from the outside.

CANDLES: As you'd expect, a lit candle brings fire energy to an area immediately. Fire is thought to encourage passion—what a surprise—and it also creates a focal point in a room. Tall white candles are recommended in Feng Shui and are best placed in the southern quarter of a room.

SOUND: It is thought that sound encourages positive chi energy. Wind chimes are popular, as is the sound of running water from a miniature inside fountain. Chimes made out of metal, wood, or ceramic are thought to enhance their coordinating elements of metal, tree, and soil. The sounds of wind chimes, bells, and ticking clocks may be used to break up stagnant energy that may be lurking under the eaves of your porch, in a dark hallway, or in those corners. The chimes should sound pleasant to you, so choose wind chimes with care. Hang them up inside; with a sweep of your hand, you can send the chimes dancing against one another and negativity scurrying right out the door.

SEA SALT: (And here I thought it was the Witches who came up with this idea.) Setting small dishes of sea salt around the home is thought to absorb negativity and bad vibes. According to Feng Shui practices, it is best poured into small white china bowls and placed in the northeast and southwest corners of the home. Remember to keep your bowls of salt out of reach from pets and small children.

AQUARIUMS: Fish bowls and aquariums are thought to encourage prosperity and to ward the home from bad luck and accidents, not to mention all the water energy they bring in to your life. Actually, watching fish swim around in an attractive aquarium is thought to help lower your blood pressure.

BOOKS: Have books arranged in clear view as you enter your home to increase insight. Wow, there must be a million insightful Wiccans and Pagans out there. Have you ever been to a magickal person's home that didn't have a ton of books everywhere?

MIRRORS: Hang up a round mirror in your bedroom to draw more love, compassion, and understanding into your romantic relationships.

FLOWERS: Arranging fresh flowers in the bedroom, kitchen, and the study or your home office encourages good luck. (You know I like this idea!)

MOVE TWENTY-SEVEN OBJECTS: Some Feng Shui experts advise that moving twenty-seven objects in your home that have not been moved in the past year will break up stagnant energy and help you to move forward with your goals and life.

Experiment with the magick of color and the power of positive energy in your home. It's fun to be magickally creative; plus, it works. If this seems too complicated for you, you can always hang up those wind chimes or a crystal sun catcher. Or you can tie a red ribbon to the inside front door—it's an old Feng Shui trick to bring about positive change and good luck.

A house is a machine for living in.

CHARLES EDOUARD JEANNERET

The Rooms Where We Live

The living or family room is most often the place where the family crashes. And to me "crashes" seems pretty darned appropriate. The family watches television or reads there. If someone is home sick they can usually be found ensconced on the couch, tucked in with blankets and riding out their cold or flu bug. In the evening, after the dishes are done, we head to the living room to flop on the sofa and unwind. We entertain there, display most of our seasonal decoration there, and this main room is the one that sees the most action, coming in second to the kitchen.

Being the most lived-in room in the house, the living/family room is also the most prone to corruption. Shoes, beverage cans, empty glasses, newspapers, magazines, and mail always seems to be found scattered across the furniture. The animals usually claim a favored chair and the kids are typically sprawled all over any available horizontal surface. There are days when I feel like I need a whip and a chair to wade my way through my living room. And, like every other mother on the planet, I am constantly after my family to "pick up their mess."

With all of this day-to-day living going on in this particular room, you might imagine it difficult to turn this mundane area into a magickal room. But actually it's very simple. First things first: try to keep the room as picked up as possible. Yes, I am aware that this is the toughest part, which is why I told you about my family just a bit ago. I live in the real world too, just like you do.

Your next step is to set up an area or workspace for natural magick supplies or accessories. Actually, I think of these as little personal altars. But the word *altar* makes some folks nervous, so call this magickal work area whatever you wish. In the living room/family room, consider choosing a place like the mantel, a wall shelf, or an end table. I would not recommend setting up on top of a television or stereo system. This is *natural* magick—let's keep it separate from the electrical energy. It could play havoc with your entertainment system. Remember that natural magick does generate power.

Also, if the thought of setting up a workspace in the living room just doesn't appeal to you, then set one up in your private space—the bedroom. Try using a nightstand or a small section on top of your dresser. How about one of those circular tables? Toss a colorful tablecloth over it and you're good to go. Maybe you can arrange some pretty celestial fabric over a TV tray and set up a portable workspace/altar there. Or use a shelf on the wall or the top of a bookshelf for something more permanent.

If you keep your magickal tools and objects as natural as possible, it merely looks like a clever arrangement of earthy, beautiful things to the casual observer. Add seasonal touches throughout the year—perhaps a small African violet in the spring, a potted fern in the summer, and so on.

At my friend Morgan's house, on the wall between her kitchen and family room, she has a small wicker shelf that is in a half circle shape. On that little shelf she tucks in a small crystal cluster and a feather. On the top shelf there is a diminutive decorative tealight candleholder in a celestial theme, a shell, and starfish. There she has all of her natural representations of the elements displayed, and she adds seasonal touches to it as the wheel of the year turns. At Lammas she had a tiny corn dolly; at Mabon, she added an apple. When our circle went to her house to celebrate the autumnal equinox, I gave her some miniature pumpkins from my garden and she tucked the littlest one up there as the holidays rolled into Samhain. At Yule, she adds sprigs of fresh holly and ivy. That little wall altar is absolutely charming.

Here are some more crafty ideas for creating magickal workspaces or altars for the rooms that we and our families live in.

> *The sum total of heaven and earth,*
> *everything in nature, is thus won to use and purpose.*
> *It becomes a temple and altar for the service of God.*
>
> HILDEGARD VON BINGEN

NATURAL MAGICK ALTARS

Create a small altar on your mantel or a shelf by adding a few subtle natural magick touches. Arrange a striking red candle into a holder and snuggle around its base smooth pebbles or sparkly crystal clusters. Scatter a few seashells within the stones to symbolize the element of water. Lastly, look for fallen feathers and tuck one or two into your display.

As you light the candle, you have all four magickal elements represented and at work within your room. If you lay claim to a wall shelf, then add taper candles at either end. Between the candles arrange your chosen natural and elemental items in a casual and pleasing way.

You can always refer to the Feng Shui practices and add a representation of each of the five elements. Try adding a piece of lucky bamboo for the wood/tree element, a silver-edged round mirror to represent the element of metal, and a small glass dish of spring water and a square terra-cotta dish filled with topsoil for the water and earth/soil elements, respectively. For the fire element, light a tall white candle.

For a more Wiccan theme, you could arrange a piece of deer antler to represent the God, and to symbolize the Goddess you could slip a rose into a vase. Try driftwood or shells for your water element, and smooth, round pebbles for earth. To represent the air element you could add a glass dish of fragrant potpourri. For the element of fire you can either use the candles or work a piece of lava rock or a chunk of volcanic glass into your display.

Perhaps you have a favorite print or artwork to use for your God and Goddess representation. Go with what you find pleasing. On the mantel in my living room there is an altar. However, it's subtle enough that most folks don't have a clue as to its actual purpose. To them it's simply an interesting arrangement of items that changes from season to season. Typically what is up there permanently includes a framed picture of the triple goddess Brigid; a small piece of deer antler that my husband found while walking out in the woods, to represent the God; a tiny cauldron—just big enough to hold a tealight; and a trio of candles. At the moment there are smaller pumpkins, autumn oak leaves, and gourds arranged across the mantel, as it's just a month away from Samhain.

Bottom line, arrange things to suit your own tastes in whichever rooms appeal to you. Perhaps you would prefer all green plants and maybe a small statue of a faerie. Believe it or not, I have that on a shelf in my bathroom. And why not, I ask you? It's the place I take ritual baths and Goddess knows the family is always in there washing their faces, brushing teeth, or fixing their hair. Seems like a good place to me for a little enchantment.

What if you wish to display your wand, ritual cup, or pentacle? Go ahead. It's your working area, after all. No matter what style you choose, bold or discreet or somewhere in between, or what theme you decide to use, just be creative and look to the environment around you for ideas and inspiration.

Here's a thought: if you live in the Southwest, then you'd probably want to include things indigenous to your area, like a small potted cactus, a dried piece of sagebrush, or a few tumbling stones of turquoise arranged in a handmade basket. A pottery dish of desert sand and another filled with spring water would be awesome. Maybe you live along the coast and you'd enjoy having seashells and starfish arranged with bleached-out, twisted pieces of driftwood. Possibly you prefer a more cottagey look . . . a pair of hand-dipped tapers in wooden candlestick holders for fire; a place to safely burn your incense and a small salt- glazed pottery bowl full of water to honor that element; another dish full of salt to represent the earth. Perhaps a hanging cluster of fragrant herbs that are drying or a rustic handmade broom that sets nearby. Both the broom and the herbs could be used to represent the element of air. See? It's easy.

Setting up this small arrangement of natural representations for each of the elements helps to keep you connected to the earth. When you incorporate natural items such as flowers, crystals, plants, stones, shells, and other seasonal fresh items into your living space, this helps to link your magick back to the beauty and wonder of nature. By celebrating these natural tools and earthy supplies of magick we honor our magickal roots. The four elements can bring many magickal energies into our lives, such as stability, creativity, enthusiasm, and love. This simple act of creating a sacred workspace to perform your spells and to connect with deity helps to connect us to the earth magicks of the cunning men and wise women from many years before.

So, now that you've got this far, why not try out one of these natural magick charms to consecrate and bless your new natural magick workspace.

FOUR ELEMENTS CONSECRATION CHARM

Set up your altar and repeat the following charm three times:

> *Earth, air, fire, and water, now combine through time and space,*
>
> *By the elements four I consecrate my working place,*
>
> *Bless all magick I perform, empower the spells that I cast,*
>
> *Create peace, harmony, and contentment that will surely last.*

Close this charm with:

> *By all the powers of land and sea,*
>
> *As I will this, then so shall it be.*

FIVE ELEMENTS CHARM

If you prefer, try this Feng Shui-style elemental charm. Repeat three times; the closing line is already worked into this charm!

> *For some, there are five elements of magickal power,*
> *Come metal, wood, fire, water, and earth, in this hour.*
> *Positive energy will flow, and darkness does now flee,*
> *Bless this Witch's home, with the power of positive chi.*

> *His house was perfect, whether you liked food,*
> *or sleep, or work, or storytelling, or singing,*
> *or a pleasant mixture of them all.*
> J. R. R. TOLKIEN, *THE HOBBIT*

WORKSPACE WITCHERY:
MAGICK FOR HOME OFFICES

A home office or workspace is a curious thing. It is a part of your home and yet it is held separate. My little office is the breezeway of our house. It started out as a small family room and has been completely taken over by my desk, computer, and bookshelves. In this room there is an old slip-covered love seat just big enough to curl up and read on, and windows that overlook part of the gardens. Is it a private space? Well, yes and no. Yes, it is private and quiet when the kids are in school, and no, it's not when they get home in the afternoon. In the evening, the kids come out here to work on papers or projects for school or to do research on the Internet.

I write every day, so I am out here in my little office seven days a week. I wake up around 5:00 AM and stagger out to the desk to get cracking before the kids get up for college and high school. Once they are up, there is no concentrating with them stomping around (unless I have headphones on). So I take a break, eat breakfast, and impatiently wait for them to clear out.

If I have to go to my part-time job, I try to get some writing in before I go to work. If I'm home for the day, I hit the computer again and then in the early afternoon I usually call it quits for the day. Since I spend so much time in this room, I wanted it to be homey. It also needed to have a good balance of practicality and comfort. And of course I wanted it to be an area that motivated me when I came to my desk to work.

So, when I decorated the office, I incorporated a touch of color magick and used warm, earthy tones to complement the knotty pine paneling in the breezeway, and added forest green curtains. Do you recall the color magick chart from earlier in this chapter? The various shades of brown are earthy, grounding colors that bring comfort, while the green is aligned to the earth element and encourages prosperity. Plus I'm a Virgo, so it all ties together. I chose my colors with care and set it up as nicely as I could. The combination of blessing the office and tying in a little color magick gave me an attractive, comfortable, and functional little office, plus it also made it inspiring and, of course, magickal.

As for accessories on the desk, I have a cluster of quartz crystals, a few framed pictures of family and friends, and a small globe of green and purple fluorite. Fluorite is a handy stone to have at your work area because it strengthens your mental powers and it is supposed to be helpful while researching and gathering information. That's a good combination for anyone to have around.

Now, it's important to point out that you don't have to have a separate room for your workstation, though that sure would be nice. Just go with whatever spot is available. Perhaps you can claim a small corner of the living room or kitchen for your workspace. I have a friend who is an artist and her magickal workspace is in the living room. She has her drawing supplies set up there, plus a few framed prints and quotes for inspiration hanging on the wall above her art table. To add a touch of magick, she adds a small lucky bamboo plant and has blue glass wind chimes hanging above her table to promote some positive chi or energy.

Occasionally she lights a small candle and sets that on her art table, and asks the Lord and Lady for inspiration. Yes, she shares the living room with her family, but this section of the room is her personal workspace. She does the bulk of her illustrations at night after her children go to bed. The important thing to realize is whether it's a private home office or just an area carved out of the family's living area, it's still your workspace. So claim it and make it into a magickal one filled with positive energy and creative vibrations.

These ideas for creating a magickal workspace at home can be easily adapted to your personal area at your job. If you have a cubicle or an office to call your very own, there are lots of clever and subtle natural magick touches that you can add. If you're going to spend a great chunk of your day at work, why not make the atmosphere a magickal one? Sometimes you only need to look at a topic from a different perspective to gain the motivation that you require. No matter if that workspace is physically within your home or across town in an office building, try adding a touch of natural magick to bring comfort and enchantment to your day.

When in doubt, follow that old Boy Scout rule of KISMIF, which stands for Keep It Simple, Make It Fun. Take another look at those Feng Shui practices for some inspiration. Hanging wind chimes above your desk and growing a small piece of lucky bamboo are subtle Feng Shui tricks that you could easily incorporate. If you'd like to slip in something from the four elements of nature at your desk, and you need to keep it low-key while on the job, no problem. Examine the altar setups that were discussed earlier in this chapter and adapt these to suit your own tastes.

Now, to close up this chapter, here is a spell to claim your workspace and to imbue it with magickal energy. You may use this on your office at home or at work.

ELEMENTAL WORKSPACE CHARM

To begin this elemental spell, sprinkle a pinch of salt around the workspace to represent the earth. Then take a cup of water and sprinkle a tiny bit around the area as well—for, you guessed it, the blessings of the water element. Visualize the heating or cooling in the room as conduits to the element of air, and the lights or the sun streaming in the windows as a representation of fire. When you are ready, repeat the charm.

> *Elements four, gather 'round this workspace of mine,*
>
> *Inspiration and comfort you bring at all times.*
>
> *Bring passion and commitment to the work that I do,*
>
> *Circle about me now with magick so strong and true.*

Close this spell with these lines:

> *By the strength of hearth and home, this spell is spun,*
>
> *As I will, so mote it be, and let it harm none.*

Chapter Three

The torch of love is lit in the kitchen.

FRENCH PROVERB

KITCHEN CUPBOARD CONJURING

While we've been covering the magickal house, you have probably noticed that I really had only skimmed over the topic of the magickal kitchen up until now. Why? Because the topic of kitchen witchery deserves its very own chapter. This often maligned magickal tradition is at the heart of cottage witchery and is practical, personal, and powerful.

There are many kitchen witches out there and to be honest, even though I don't like to get stuck cooking dinner, I do enjoy whipping up a little magick in the kitchen with culinary herbs and spices from time to time. Kitchen magick is unique in that it can be applied to any magickal tradition or path. When you practice kitchen magick, you get the opportunity to put your own creative spin on things.

In many homes throughout history the kitchen held a place of honor. By tradition, most of the work of the wise woman took place or began at the hearth. Today, the hearth is the kitchen—this isn't too hard to visualize, as more and more folks spend family time in the kitchen. Kids do their homework there, family meetings are held around the table, and at a party everyone gravitates toward the kitchen.

However, the mood or feeling of a kitchen changes when it is used for magick. There is a subtle but strong magickal atmosphere in an enchanted kitchen. For many practitioners this is the most practical spot in which to work their magick, since herbs and spices are right at hand. And there are a variety of common spices and seasonings that can double as magickal herbs. The trick is to look at them and use them in a whole new way.

A good cook is like a sorceress who dispenses happiness.

ELISA SCHIAPARELLI

SPICE RACK SORCERY

Various common kitchen spices, extracts, and seasonings pack a wallop of magickal power when worked into charms and spells. You'd be amazed at what kinds of enchantments you can create just by working with common kitchen spices, seasonings, and cooking herbs. Check out this Witch's list, and this chapter's following kitchen magick information, and see what sort of personalized spells and charms you can cook up.

ALLSPICE: money and good luck

BASIL: wealth and good luck

BAY LEAF: purification, health, and strength

CHIVES: protection, absorbs bad vibes

CINNAMON: prosperity, happy homes

CLOVES: protection, stops gossip

DILL: security, money; frightens away unwanted creatures

GARLIC: protection, purification, exorcism

GINGER: power and prosperity

LEMON/LEMON RIND: breaks up negativity, healing

MACE: increases psychic powers

MINT (LEAVES): prosperity and protection

MUSTARD SEED: fertility and safe houses

ORANGE RIND: energy, vitality, and health

PARSLEY: purification, protection

PEPPERMINT EXTRACT: cleansing, purification, and protection

ROSEMARY: healing, love

SAGE: wisdom

THYME: sleep, courage; promotes good health

VANILLA EXTRACT: love, passion; stimulates mental powers

Oh, who can tell the hidden power of herbs

and might of magic spell.

EDMUND SPENSER

CREATING HERBAL MAGICK
IN THE KITCHEN

The kitchen is often the center of the home. There is no reason why it cannot be a magickal room as well. Clean out a small section of kitchen cupboard, up and out of reach of young children. Then arrange a few natural magick supplies like candles, crystals, and herbs in there. Perhaps you can set an attractive tealight candleholder back on the counter to have handy for magick. Then the next time you're preparing dinner, or riding herd on the kids and their homework, you can also be working a quick kitchen magick spell.

ALL-PURPOSE KITCHEN MAGICK CHARM

Here is a quick all-purpose charm to go along with your "spicy" kitchen magick.

Enchanted kitchen herbs of brown and green,

Spellcraft can be simpler than it seems.

Add these herbs for power and magick true,

Goddess bless my spells and all that I do.

Close the charm with:

> *For the good of all, with harm to none,*
> *With spices and herbs, this spell is done!*

Think of all the quick and easy spells you could perform with this all-purpose charm. Tie magickal spices into a small fabric charm bag and carry it with you—dill seeds and allspice to promote prosperity, for example. What about a clove of garlic and a sprig of parsley for purification and protection?

Using an old teapot, try steeping a few of the herbal ingredients in water on the stove and letting the scent permeate the air and the atmosphere in the home. Good, sweet-smelling choices for steeping would be lemon rind to break up negativity, cinnamon for prosperity, and cloves to stop gossip.

You could also sprinkle a bit of herb on an unlit tealight candle. That way, as you light the spell candle, you're adding the extra punch of herbal magick to an otherwise simple candle spell.

PRACTICAL MAGICK WITH THE ALL-PURPOSE TEALIGHT

The tealight candle is a sensible solution to expensive beeswax tapers and pillar candles. Tealight candles are available in packages of twelve for usually under two dollars, and they can also be purchased in bags of fifty. Watch for them to go on sale and snag a big bag to keep on hand for candle spells. I don't know about you, but no matter how hard I try, I always seem to be out of a specific color for a candle spell.

I rely on tealight magick a lot. Between running my two teenagers to their sports or band practices, attending various school functions, checking in on my oldest son (the college student), volunteering with the Master Gardeners, and keeping up with my gardens, this leaves me with very little time to go on the hunt for high-priced specialty candles. These little babies are a practical solution.

Tealights are perfect for herbal candle spells. They burn for about four hours and are typically white and unscented. (Don't forget that white is an all-purpose magickal color.) If you would prefer to have them scented, you can always add a drop of essential oil on them that could coordinate with your magickal intention, like clove oil for protection or cinnamon oil for prosperity. Try sweet orange oil to revitalize and refresh yourself after a long day. You could also try adding a drop of vanilla extract on the candle—vanilla encourages mental powers, love, and desire. Or simply do as suggested previously and sprinkle a little bit of one of those magickal spices on top of the unlit candle or in the bottom of the metal cup. Slipping it into the bottom of the cup is neater and very discreet. Place the tealight on top of the herbs and you are ready to cast.

TEALIGHT PETITION MAGICK

If you wish to perform petition magic with a tealight, then write the request on a small piece of paper, fold it up, and tuck it neatly beneath the tealight, in the bottom of the little metal candle cup. Add a pinch of your corresponding herb to the cup, replace the candle, light it, and work your spell. When the candle is finished burning, you will notice that your slip of paper is sealed to the bottom of the cup and covered in wax. Your spell is safely sealed and you may now dispose of the little metal candle cup in the garbage. Here is a quick candle charm to go along with your herbal candle magic.

Tealight candle burning warm and bright,

Lend your magick to me on this night.

Herbs and spices add strength and magical power

Goddess, bless my work in this enchanted hour.

Tealights are also available in many colors and scents. If you prefer to use these as opposed to the plain variety, then refer to the color magick chart from chapter 2 (it's a good general guide for color magick). Remember while working your candle magick to never leave those candles unattended. If you must, then move them to the bottom of an empty sink to finish burning.

The tealight candle is a great, affordable accessory to any type of spellwork or charm. Candlelight adds its own magickal atmosphere. Most Witches work with candle magick quite regularly. Candles, in all of their various shapes, colors, and sizes, add the extra push of the element of fire and bring more passion and enthusiasm into your spellwork. Often one of the first magickal techniques learned, it is up to you to decide how to incorporate this information into the Craft that you already practice. Experiment with adding a tealight candle to these next practical kitchen charms.

Making the simple complicated is commonplace;

making the complicated simple, awesomely

simple, that's creativity.

CHARLES MINGUS

SIMPLE KITCHEN MAGICK

You want fast, quick, and simple spells and charms? Try working a little easy kitchen magick and see what you can create. Take the following ideas and adapt them for your own purposes. By adding your own flair, this will personalize the spells and make them uniquely your own. Most of the ingredients for the following kitchen charms are common and readily available. Rummage around the kitchen cabinets—I bet you have many of the supplies already.

Please use natural cooking supplies and dishes or containers whenever possible. Glass, wood, and ceramicware are much more conducive to natural magick energies than plastic. Metal bowls or trays will also work (remember that metal is one of the five elements of Feng Shui). If salt is called for in a spell, you may use sea salt or table salt, whatever you have handy or would prefer.

As you close up and bind these kitchen charms and spells, try using this oldie but goodie standard closing line:

By all the powers of three times three,

As I will it, so shall it be.

Sure, this magickal line is used all of the time. It's a good one. By saying this closing line you are verbally reinforcing that you accept and embrace the idea of karma. You are also stating that you are working positive magick and that you embrace the Rule of Three.

A JUICY SPELL FOR REMOVING BAD VIBES

To remove sour feelings and bad vibes, take a small glass bowl, ceramic dish, or coffee mug and sprinkle a few inches of salt in the bottom. Next squirt a bit of lemon juice on top of the salt. Say:

> *Lemon juice and white salt, by mixing thee*
> *No bad vibes will cling or hang around me.*
> *Remove all the negativity and despair*
> *By the powers of earth, water, fire, and air.*

SWEET PROSPERITY SPELL

Mix together a teaspoon of cinnamon for prosperity, a teaspoon of allspice to bring money, and a half cup of sugar to sweeten up your life. Mix the ingredients together, then pour into a glass container. Snap or screw the lid into place. Empower the mixture to bring prosperity into your life. Try this charm:

> *Sugar and spice and everything nice,*
> *Make up this Witch's spell,*
> *A pinch of magick, a bit of charm,*
> *And all will turn out well.*

You could put a pinch of this mixture into a charm bag, or seal a tablespoon of it inside an envelope and keep it in your bill drawer or the bottom of your purse to promote prosperity. Or just sprinkle a spoonful on your buttered toast in the morning to add prosperity and success to your day.

PROTECTION CHARM BAG

Garlic is a great protective herb. Besides its supposed properties of keeping away vampires and the roaming undead, a clove of garlic comes in handy for kitchen magick. For this kitchen charm, use a four-inch square of black fabric and about six to eight inches of black ribbon. Place the clove of garlic for protection and purification in the center of the fabric. Add a pinch of salt to break up any negativity you feel may be surrounding you or the situation.

Gather up each edge of the square, naming them for each of the four elements. After you gather the corners together, tie the bag closed with the ribbon. Take a careful look at this kitchen charm, the directions are all laid out for you.

By *the powers of earth* (pick up one corner)

And *air* (gather the second corner)

And *fire* (pick up the third)

And *water* (add the last corner)

I *create this Witch's protective charm.*

(tie the fabric closed with the ribbon)

Grant me safety and shield me from all harm.

Remember to seal this charm with the closing line,

> By *all the powers of three times three,*
> As I *will it, then so shall it be.*

You may keep the charm bag on your person or tucked away in the most-used room of your home to boost your magickal household protections.

APPLES OF KNOWLEDGE SPELL

For this divinatory spell you'll need your divinatory tools (tarot cards, runes, etc.), an apple, and a pinch of mace. Mace is a great-tasting spice to add to old-fashioned and country apple dishes and recipes. Apples have long been considered magickal fruits. Their associations run the gambit from love to divination to healing. Slice the apple crosswise to reveal the star that is hidden inside. Dust the apple with a pinch of mace to encourage psychic powers. Place the apple pieces inside of a bowl and intone the following divinatory charm:

> *Apples of red, green, and gold,*
> *Show me what my future holds.*
> *Mace is a spice that encourages foresight,*
> *Help this kitchen witch's spell to turn out right.*

Now cast your runes or deal out your tarot cards. When you are finished with this kitchen charm, leave the apple neatly outside for nature to reclaim. Or you could eat the apple for a snack, thus taking the power of foresight and knowledge into yourself.

For more ideas on kitchen divination, check out our next section. Have you ever considered trying your hand at tea-leaf reading?

Tell me, Gypsy, what can you see in my cup of tea?

Can you predict my future, tell me my past?

ANONYMOUS

READING TEA LEAVES

Tea-leaf reading was a popular pastime in England, Scotland, Ireland, and in Victorian-era America. Also known as tasseography, tea-leaf reading was probably one of the more popular forms of divination practiced a century or two ago. To perform tea-leaf reading you need to start with a fresh pot of tea. First brew up some loose tea in a pot and pour the unstrained tea into each cup. It is recommended that you use plain china cups for tea-leaf reading, as a patterned cup makes the shapes harder to discern. This would be fun to do at a circle meeting, an old-fashioned Halloween party, or a Samhain get-together with your magickal friends. Try this out and see what kind of results you get.

Have the questioner drink the tea until the liquid is almost gone. Then take the cup and turn it around deosil (that's clockwise) three times while saying the following charm:

Great Goddess, show me love, happiness, and good luck

As I divine the future within this teacup.

By all the powers of three times three,

As I will it, then so shall it be.

Turn the cup over and onto the saucer and allow the remaining tea to drain out. Now you're ready to read. Look for shapes made by the leaves—use your imagination! Leaves that are closer to the rim of the cup show events in the immediate future. Leaves deeper into the cup or at the bottom indicate events in the distant future. Likewise, the handle of the teacup is important in the reading as well. How close the shapes are to the handle tells you how close these events are to occurring.

TEA-LEAF SYMBOLS AND THEIR MEANINGS

ANCHOR: travel

BELL: good news

BUTTERFLY: happiness

CANDLE: illumination

CAT: secrets

CRESCENT MOON: Goddess and moon magick

CUP: emotions and psychic abilities

DOG: loyalty

EGG: pregnancy

EYE: protection

FLOWER: happiness and admiration

HAND: help is on the way

HEART: love

HOUSE: security

HORSE: stamina

KEY: opportunity and knowledge

LADDER: promotion at work

LEAF: Green Man and earth magick

QUESTION MARK: uncertainty

RING: marriage

SNAKE: gossip and hurt feelings

STAR: magick

TREE: good luck and success

Remember that just like other divinatory tools, such as the runes or the tarot, tea-leaf readings are open to personal interpretation. Feel free to include your own personal symbolic meanings to other shapes that are not listed here. Also, more than one shape within the cup can make for a more interesting reading, as both the symbols must be interpreted by how they affect each other—such as a question mark and a ring popping up in the same cup. Marriage may indeed be a part of the questioner's future, but how do they feel about it? Are they uncertain? Another school of thought is that clear shapes distinguish good luck while vague shapes indicate an unclear outcome and delay. This type of divinatory reading takes some practice. I guess you'd better break out some fancy cookies, brew up a pot of fragrant tea, and start practicing!

I am beginning to learn that it is the sweet,

simple things of life which are the real ones after all.

LAURA INGALLS WILDER

COTTAGE WITCHERY IN THE KITCHEN

How do you go about working cottage witchery in the kitchen? Well, I just grab my trusty jars of dried garden herbs and gather a few fresh magickal flowers. Then I dig through my kitchen spices and seasonings and conjure up a little magick. I work out a quick charm or spell and use my imagination and typically I keep things very simple. A small candle, herbs, flowers, and occasionally a wooden spoon that doubles for a wand. If I am not working or digging in the garden, there is a good chance I'm stirring up some natural magick in the kitchen.

Some supplies to keep on hand for natural kitchen magick would be a vase for garden flowers and fresh herbal foliage; a candle holder and some plain tealights; assorted glass storage jars for your various dried magickal herbs and flowers; small glass, ceramic, or wooden bowls; a small cauldron or an old cooking pot; and a wooden spoon. You could cast or conjure with this wooden spoon, create a circle, or stir up your herbal ingredients.

Now, before someone even starts complaining, there is *nothing* demeaning about using a wooden spoon in kitchen magick! I have a decorative antique wooden spoon that I keep in a crock on the kitchen counter. (I don't use it in food preparation.) In a pinch it makes for a great wand. For example, when my kids were small and I was working a little magick at the counter while doing the mundane chores of cooking and cleaning, I would use that spoon to direct the energy where I wanted it to go. You know, just point, aim, and shoot? Hey, don't knock it. It always worked for me.

So here I am, barefoot, in jeans and a T-shirt, daring to conjure up simple, natural magicks with what I have on hand. I know it blows my image not to be flouncing about in ritual wear 24/7, but the majority of the time when I work my magick I am in street clothes. (Shocking, isn't it?) Don't even try and convince me that most Witches work in ceremonial robes every day of the week. Let's be realistic.

It is not what you wear, or how many fancy ritual accessories that you own, that makes you into a creative and powerful Witch. It's how you use and work with the natural supplies and the down-to-earth magickal tools that you do have. How do you interact with the magickal environment that is around you? What sort of magickal energy radiates from your home? All of this makes for very personal and individualized magick. It also helps to remind us that every Witch is unique. We should celebrate this and refine our techniques. This is what makes magick powerful. Hence the idea for cottage witchery was born.

Write your own spells, come up with your own custom-made charms. Just do your own thing. If you're wondering where to start, I'm about to give you a spell worksheet to help you organize and create your own simple natural spells and kitchen magick. Check this worksheet out for yourself; refer to the information and simple kitchen supplies that were featured in this chapter. Just imagine all of the spicy spells and charms you can whip up!

For more information on garden flowers to use in natural magick, check out my previous book, *Garden Witchery*. It's crammed full of gardening information and easy-to-grow magickal flowers and herbs that incorporate nicely into natural magick and kitchen witch charms and spells.

Natural Kitchen Magick Worksheet

GOAL: _____
_____
_____

KITCHEN SPICES USED: _____
_____
_____

MAGICKAL SIGNIFICANCE OF THE SPICES: _____
_____
_____

CANDLE COLOR (FOR CANDLE MAGICK): _____
_____
_____

FRESH HERBS OR GARDEN FLOWERS: _____
_____
_____

CHARM OR VERSE: _____
_____
_____
_____
_____

FUN KITCHEN FOLKLORE

In closing up this chapter, I thought a touch of folklore would be just the thing. Folklore and old country superstitions are a treasure-trove full of magickal lore and fun. Some of this information could be used in practical magick and some is just for your enjoyment.

Kitchen folklore states that bubbles appearing in your coffee cup signal that money is on the way. Likewise for knocking over the sugar bowl, rice that forms a ring around the cooking pot, and tea leaves that float to the top of the teacup.

Visitors are coming to your home if cutlery drops to the floor; a fork signifies a man, and a spoon a woman. In the Ozarks it's a fork for a fellow and a knife for a lady. If a glass falls to the floor but does not break, it is an indication of true and trustworthy friends. There is the old-time belief, revitalized by the movie *Practical Magic*, that if a broom falls over, company is coming. Also, if you prop your kitchen broom up against the doorframe, it keeps all troublesome family members or unwanted visitors out.

Here is another little gem of kitchen magick: scattering mustard seeds across the threshold was thought to keep out unwanted guests. To keep away spirits you are supposed to bury mustard seeds under your doorway or porch.

According to Ozark folklore, if a woman drops the dishrag on the floor, that is bad luck. This bad luck can be removed by throwing a pinch of salt over her shoulder. Some texts claim that you should bury the dishrag. Personally, I'd just throw it in the washing machine and bleach it. Empower the bleach to kill germs and to clean up any bad vibes, raging teenage hormones and melodramas, or negativity that might be hanging around the house.

In the old days it was thought that a "bad woman could not make good applesauce." Sneezing before breakfast signals visitors before noon. Sneezing while eating breakfast is a sign that you'll have two visitors leaving before sunset. Oh, and if you sneeze on a Monday, you're sure to kiss a stranger before the week is out!

Spilling water on the tablecloth was supposed to signify rainstorms. Ditto for a coffeepot that boils over again and again. And should your kitchen apron come untied all by itself and fall to the floor while you're in the kitchen, your lover is believed to be entertaining some rather *intense* romantic thoughts about you.

All in all, the kitchen is a hotbed of magickal activity. It can be a charming room and a magickal workspace where enchantment, practicality, and everyday life go hand in hand. So live and work in this room with magickal intention. Dare to stir up your herbal and spicy spells with a special wooden spoon—go deosil (clockwise) to increase and to pull positive things into your life, and stir widdershins (counterclockwise) to remove obstacles and negativity. Work cottage witchery charms in the kitchen with conviction and magickal purpose. I'll bet that you'll create something magickal every day.

Take the information that was presented in this chapter and adapt it to suit your own magickal needs. And be yourself. Remember . . . magick is where you find it, and creativity is the key.

Chapter Four

Come, Vesta, to live in this beautiful home.

Come with your warm feelings of friendship.

Bring your intelligence, your energy, and your passion

to join with your good work. Burn always in my soul.

You are welcome here. I remember you.

—HOMERIC HYMN (TRANSLATION BY
FRANCES BERNSTEIN)

DEITIES, FAERIES, AND MAGICK OF THE HEARTH FLAME

The deities of the hearth are warm and inviting goddesses. These ladies symbolize the comforts, strengths, and loving magick of the home. The three goddesses that we will focus on here are traditional keepers of the hearth flame and the personification of the enchanting spirit of the magickal home.

Hestia and Vesta: The Sacred Flame

Hestia, or Vesta, was the Greco-Roman goddess of the hearth. Hestia was known as the "first of all divinities to be invoked." Hestia was the oldest of her sisters, Demeter and Hera, but there are not a lot of mythological tales about Hestia as she was always tending the flame, whether it was in Olympus or the hearth fire of the ancient home. Hestia, called the "one of light," was embodied by the flame—so there are few representations or images of this hearth-flame goddess. According to the ancient magician Pythagoras, the fire of Hestia's hearth was the center of the earth because she literally *was* the flame. Hestia represented the unity of family and state, hospitality, and the spiritual center of the home.

Vesta was the Roman equivalent of the Greek goddess Hestia. In Rome, Vesta's sacred flames were tended by the vestal virgins. The vestal virgins were thought to have served for thirty years, beginning their term in childhood. Afterwards, they were free to marry or remain within the ranks. The vestal virgins wielded quite a bit of political clout in their time. Should a condemned man happen to met a vestal virgin in the street, he was set free. The vestal virgins were protected and there were many dire consequences for accidentally injuring or harming a priestess of Vesta.

There is another school of thought that believes the vestal virgins may not have been "virgins" at all. They may have been a virgin in the sense of the word that they belonged to no one but themselves. They may have been free to choose their sexual partners at the temple. Lying with a priestess of Vesta may have been like being with the goddess herself. It wouldn't be the first time in history that men sought out the priestesses at the temples for sacred sex. It also may help to explain why the church was so eager to shut them down.

The goddess Vesta did have a couple of special days. One was March 2. This first festival was a day reserved for cleaning and purifying the temple and lighting a new ceremonial fire. Another festival called the Vestalia was celebrated on June 7. There were in later times a few images of Vesta found on Roman coins. Typically she was depicted as a veiled woman bearing a torch and a scepter. These vestal priestesses tended the eternal fire up until the sixth century, until the church acquired enough power to oust the priestesses of Vesta and remove their political and religious rights.

Hestia and Vesta were both significant goddesses, since in ancient times the hearth was a sacred place. Fire keeping, creating the food, and tending a home and family were among the most revered of tasks. As all of these activities centered around the hearth flame, Hestia and Vesta were an integral part of ancient home life. While Hestia may have been more of a quiet domestic-goddess type, she was still a revered one. Vesta's worship was more organized, political, and, some believe, sexual. Either way, they were both influential and powerful goddesses of their time. Symbols for Hestia and Vesta include the color red, the astrological symbol for the asteroid Vesta (-⚶-), burning candles, a cauldron, the fireplace hearth, and, of course, fire.

May the blessed sun shine upon you and warm your
heart until it glows like a great peat fire—so that the
stranger may come and warm himself, also a friend.

IRISH BLESSING

BRIGID: THE BRIGHT ONE

The triple goddess Brigid is known by many names: Bride, Brigit, Brighid, and Brigitania. The Celtic pronunciation of her name is *breed*. A popular goddess with Witches, Pagans, and Druids, she is occasionally referred to as the patroness of the bards, the "bright one," the "bright arrow," the Flame of Ireland, or the Triple Brigits. This titan-haired goddess of the flame and the hearth fire was important in the Celtic pantheon. Brigid was the daughter of the Dagda, and Celtic mythology claims that when she was born, a tower of flame rose from the crown of her head straight up into the heavens. The light was so bright it was thought that the cottage where she was born might be on fire.

The household fire was also sacred to Brigid, and she was often depicted as either holding flames within the palms of her hands or being surrounded by a fiery halo of light. Brigid is traditionally a goddess of smithcraft, poetry, and healing. And if you think about it for a moment, the traditional magickal aspects of this triple goddess are all related to the element of fire. A smith needs heat and flame to create his iron and steel. A poet calls on her inner fire for inspiration, and a healer works with the energy of fire for transformation to bring about a positive change and a healthier patient.

To keep things interesting, Brigid is also associated with sacred wells and springs. (Probably due in part to her association with healing.) Among the many qualities this goddess presides over are childbirth, fertility, arts and crafts, education, and psychic abilities. However, her position as a deity of the hearth is in the forefront. Similar to Vesta, Brigid also had priestesses (some say nine, others insist nineteen) who tended her eternal flame in Kildare, Ireland.

Brigid's sacred day is the Sabbat of Imbolc celebrated on February 1 or 2, depending on the magickal tradition. Off the coast of Scotland, in the Hebrides Islands, there is a festival for Brigid called Lá Fheill Brighid. On this day the female head of the house chants over and blesses an image of the goddess Brigid. The dolly is typically made of straw or corn husks and is dressed in maiden white. A crystal is placed over the dolly's heart and she is placed in a cradle-style basket. This annual ceremony invites the spirit of the goddess Brigid into the home and asks for her blessing for the coming year.

Imbolc is a major Sabbat in the Wiccan tradition and is also known as Candlemas. It marks the cross-quarter day and halfway point of winter and spring. Symbols for Brigid include snakes, swans, milk, purple spring crocus, the white snowdrop, a blacksmith forge, a cauldron, a four-spoke cross made from rushes (called a Brigid's cross), white stones, three intertwined circles, the number nine, and the triple goddess colors of white, red, and black.

A HEARTH GODDESS CHARM

To invoke the benevolence of the hearth goddesses and invite these deities into your home, try this candle charm. Even if you don't have a fireplace, you can still re-create a miniature hearth. Find a safe, flat surface to set up on and make your own magickal hearth area. Feel free to work this charm at any time throughout the year: at sunrise, the full moon, a new crescent moon, or at one of the major Sabbats. When you light this candle and say these words, you are calling in the goddesses to protect and watch over you. Basically you are welcoming these ladies into your life. See what sort of stability, warmth, and enchantment they bring to your days.

Gather these supplies:

* One red pillar candle

* A candleholder or small plate

* Nine white, small, smooth stones

* A pinch of salt

* A lighter or matches

Arrange the nine white stones around a red pillar candle and its holder. Dust the stones with a pinch of salt to consecrate them. Take a moment to visualize your miniature hearth. See it glowing with warmth, magick, and hospitality. Light the candle and repeat the following charm three times:

> Goddesses of the home and the sacred hearth flame,
> Brigid, Hestia, and Vesta, I call your names.
> A candle for fire, a ring of stones becomes your hearth,
> Bless us with warmth and security from this Witch's art.

Close the spell:

> By all the powers of the earth and fire,
> This spell is sealed by my will and desire.

Allow the candle to burn for a few hours. When you are finished, snuff the candle and relight it whenever you feel the need to reconnect to the goddesses of the hearth and home.

> I am of a little world made cunningly
> of elements, and an angelic sprite.
> JOHN DONNE

HOUSEHOLD FAERIES: THE BROWNIES

Tell folks that you believe in the faeries, and that will get you some very strong reactions. Tell them you've seen the faeries and they'll wonder how to get you into therapy. Others will look at you with very wide eyes and make a condescending remark, or they think you're teasing them. Some people may believe you. Others may be comfortable with this thought because they imagine a stylized, popular culture's rendition of faeries and picture a type of romantic earthbound angel. I think that mindset comes from an old European legend that the Fae may be angels who were bound to the earth for not choosing sides during the big rebellion in heaven.

However, what we are speaking of here is the more classic folktale-type of elemental spirit. These characters are more earthy and elemental than romantic and imaginary. The faery realm is within our reach, it just takes a different level of sensitivity to experience it. For this type of natural magick you need an open mind, a loving heart, and a willingness to believe. Oh—and enough common sense to keep yourself out of trouble.

These faery or elemental energies are discernable, but you are much more likely to sense the faeries long before you ever catch a glimpse of them. Still, it doesn't hurt to have the lay of the land, so to speak, when it comes to common house faeries and elemental beings.

I once had a problem with the household spirits, or faeries—whichever term you prefer. I thought it would be fun to invite them in, just to see if it would really work. Okay, I admit it. I was a novice Witch, young and cocky. Boy, did it work. I landed myself a crash course in faery etiquette from that experience. Bottom line: know who you're inviting before you go and open up that magickal door into your home. And be prepared for the consequences. With the faery kingdom, there is no such thing as a free lunch.

Someone once asked me how the faeries ended up over here in the States if they are indigenous to Europe. Well, my two cents' worth on this topic is this: they either traveled with their families when the families immigrated to America, or another possibility is that elemental creatures are everywhere, in every continent. They may have different names, but the energy and the spirit of the faeries are *everywhere* in nature. So why wouldn't they be here? The land our homes stand upon was a wilderness at one time or another. Why would the elemental spirits of the land and the energies of nature leave? Perhaps they have only been hiding and waiting for you to notice them all along.

One of the most common faeries and elemental beings that may find their way into your magickal home is the brownie. There are many different varieties of brownies, from many magickal cultures in all parts of the world.

The brownies are thought to vary in height and in their appearance. The Scottish version of the brownie calls for them to be one to two feet tall. Other texts claim that they are only six to twelve inches in height, wearing brown cloaks or hoods or fur tunics. Typically the brownies are small, furry, and . . . well, brown. This household faery was thought to have completed unfinished household tasks.

The brownies love animals, family pets, and the noise and activity of children. Actually, your pets will notice the presence of brownies long before you do, especially cats. Your cat will happily pounce, hop, and prance around for no apparent reason. Supposedly when they do this they are playing with the house faeries.

Hobs or hobgoblins are an English version of the brownie, and they are another house faery known for making their home behind the kitchen stove or the family fireplace or hearth area. A hobgoblin is thought of as the spirit of the hearth, or guardian of the fireside. Once settled with their adoptive family, the hob rarely leaves, which may be why some came along with their beloved immigrating families as opposed to staying behind. Hobs are happiest tending to their chosen family and helping out with whatever they perceive as being their daily chores. If a hob feels unwanted or ignored, they are likely to hide your key rings and place them in very unusual places. Puck, who made a appearance in a charm in our first chapter, is a hobgoblin.

The Bwca is a Welsh name for the brownie; the Bwca can be very helpful around the home unless they are angered, and then they can become destructive. So what does it take to really tick off a brownie? Quite a bit, actually, such as ignoring them or saying out loud that you don't believe in household faeries, or undergoing a major household renovation or remodel. If you have one planned you may want to enlist the help of your household faeries. Ask them to keep an eye on things and, as strange as this sounds, let them know what the plans are for the remodel. Otherwise they'll see this as the destruction of their beloved home and do everything they can to slow the process down.

Delays, strange equipment mishaps, and snafus will be your constant companions. (That's what happened to my family.) I finally had to leave my renovation plans out and on the hearth overnight with a few small crystal points for the brownies. That night I dreamt about them checking out the plans with our cat and discussing it amongst themselves. In the morning when I got up, the gifts were gone and the plan was still on the hearth. My old tabby cat was sitting guard next to it.

Brownie temper tantrums can include throwing things (I would imagine some would see this as poltergeist activity); hiding valuables such as jewelry, wallets, or keys; spoiling the milk; and, according to tradition, making the beer go stale or flat.

To pacify them, the brownies all enjoy attention and gifts. Try offering a crystal point, or milk and honey, or a plain cookie. Brownies are thought to be offended by an offer of money or clothing. For the most part, brownies in all of their various names and nationalities are happiest quietly tending to their beloved family and helping out around the hearth and home. To keep them happy, try whispering this charm at night before you head off to bed.

A HOUSE FAERY CHARM

Go through your usual evening routine. For me that includes one last trip through the living room and kitchen to tidy up and make sure all the doors are locked, all the lights are turned out, and any burning candles have been snuffed. Then, as you are ready to turn in, go to the heart of the home and quietly whisper this charm.

> *Beloved brownies and faeries of my house,*
> *I whisper my thanks, as quiet as a mouse.*
> *Watch over my family, protect my pets,*
> *Thank you for your help as I go off to rest.*

Close the charm by saying:

> *By the hearth and home this charm is sung,*
> *For the good of all, with harm to none.*

Go where he will, the wise man is at home,

His hearth the earth, his hall the azure dome.

R. W. EMERSON

FIREPLACE/HEARTH MAGICK

In Roman times the family hearth was designated by the Latin word *focus*. It was the heart of clan and tribal life. Sacred to the goddesses such as Brigid, Hestia, and Vesta, the hearth fire was presided over by the family matriarch. Her task was an essential one, as the fire was a living symbol of the family's spirit.

In magick, fire is the element of transformation. There is something magickal about working your spells and charms by the light of a fireplace or in the flickering illumination of candles. Fire is a magickal mood enhancer; it's powerful, destructive, and creative, all at the same time. Working by the hearth with your fireplace or wood-burning stove is a way to link your magick back to the ways of the village Witch, cunning man, or wise woman. It is also a golden opportunity to get to know and to work with the salamanders, the fire elementals. If you do not have a fireplace, don't fret. Simply create your own hearthstone with a trio of tall pillar candles and a few decorative flat stones arranged around them in a semicircle, similar to what was suggested in the hearth goddess charm. Consecrate these hearthstones with a pinch of salt or a drop of essential oil. Make sure that wherever you arrange this, it is well away from flammable items like curtains and upholstery.

Give me a spark o' Nature's fire,

That's all the learning I desire.

ROBERT BURNS

SALAMANDERS AND SCRYING WITH FIRE

Salamanders are the elemental embodiment of fire. Without the energies and powers of the salamanders, fire would not exist. Salamanders are often described as being small lizards or glowing, reddish-gold balls of flaming light. Salamanders are loyal and quick to protect their families. The salamanders, like their elemental cousins the dragons and the firedrakes, are all part of the elemental world of fire. The gifts they bestow upon us are warmth, passion, enthusiasm, and the psychic ability to "see." If you care to try and work with the fire elementals, then try your hand at scrying with fire.

Scrying with fire is called pyromancy. This technique can be difficult for a beginner, but that's usually because they are thinking the process to death. If you have a fire in the fireplace, merrily crackling away, then lay down on the floor in front of your hearth on your belly and get comfortable. Rest your chin on your hands and settle in to watch the flames. Now let your mind drift and your imagination go. Let your eyes unfocus and blink naturally. What sort of pictures do you see in the flames?

A house may symbolize prosperity. Trees and horseshoes are thought to mean success, good luck, and prosperity. A horse, plane, or ship signifies a journey, and a flying bird means that a letter is on the way. A bell is an omen for a wedding and a cradle portends a baby.

Relax and enjoy yourself as you gaze into the flames—but try not to fall asleep. If you don't have a fireplace or stove, then use your candle and hearthstone setup. Just let your vision blur and your mind drift as you watch the candle flames. Give yourself about a half hour for your first attempt, and note down any impressions or images that you see.

If you have lots of sparks popping against the fireplace or stove screen while you are scrying, that is usually a good sign that the salamanders are trying to work with you. If you have big billows of smoke and tall flames that suddenly flare up, then the dragons and drakes are on the job. If for some reason the fire begins to smolder out, then give it a prod and feed it more wood. Don't panic if the flames peter out on you, just stoke the fire back up and enjoy the process.

If you are using candle flames to scry, then watch those carefully as well. Crackling or chattering candles mean the salamanders are close. Tall or dancing candle flames (that are not caused by a draft or breeze) indicate the energies of the drakes and dragons.

Here is another option for those of you without a fireplace. Try burning a candle inside of a cast-iron cauldron. This simple and practical act can re-create a touch of cottage witchery-style hearth magick. After all, what's a Witch's cottage without a cauldron?

Should your candle flames take on a blue tinge, that is thought to represent the presence of a ghost. Now, should this happen, and it makes you uncomfortable, call on any of our previously mentioned hearth goddesses and the fire elementals for their assistance. Sprinkle a bit of salt at each of the four corners of your home and ask that the spirit move on to a happier place.

Flame of magic, brightly burn, spirit of the fire.

Let the wheel of fortune turn, grant me my desire.

DOREEN VALIENTE

FIRE MAGICK

In keeping with our natural magick theme, let's take a closer look at fire magick. Fire is one of the more powerful natural elements. Candle spells are pretty much a starting point for most beginners, and most magickal books feature at least a handful of candle spells (this book is no exception). Back in chapter 2 there was a color correspondence chart that may certainly be used for candle magick as well. However, I want to give you something different to try—something more time-honored and more in keeping with the traditions of the old wise ones.

To work this type of enchantment you are going to need an open flame, either from a fireplace, a wood stove, or an outdoor old-style barbecue pit. How about one of those new metal portable outdoor fire pits with the screens all around? I have used an old kettle-type of barbecue grill with sticks and kindling arranged inside of it. It's safe, and the flames are contained and well above the ground. Its black color and shape reminded me of a cauldron.

My group has used this setup for a midsummer's miniature bonfire in my backyard. We all took turns tossing into the flames various herbs and magickal flowers from my gardens. While we did, we each made a wish for prosperity or health during the dark half of the year. It was a complete surprise to us that those green, fresh herbs made sparks and the color of the flames changed. Maybe it was the addition of green material into the fire, or perhaps it was simply the magick of a circle of Witches celebrating the summer solstice.

If you do build a small outdoor fire, please be safe and smart. Keep water and hoses at the ready. Also make sure that long, dangling sleeves or unbound hair is kept well out of harm's way.

Crumple up some newspaper and place it in the center of the fire pit. Arrange your small sticks and dry kindling in a teepee shape. Stack a few slightly larger pieces of wood on top of your sticks and kindling—about three or four pieces leaning together ought to do the trick. (Generally you'll want this spell-fire to burn for about a half hour, so keep your stack of sticks and kindling on the small side.) Use a long wooden match or lighter to light the paper on fire. Once you've built a nice small fire and it's crackling away, you can try these following fire spells and charms.

AN HERBAL BLESSING FOR LOVE AND WISDOM

For this fire spell you will need the following herbal ingredients. You may use dried or fresh.

* A handful of lavender buds

* A blossom or two of yarrow

* A few red rose petals

Repeat the charm below, carefully adding each of these herbal ingredients into the fire. Look over the spell before you begin. The directions are within the spell.

Lavender buds bring protection and love,

Goddess, hear my call, answer from above. (Toss in the lavender.)

A cluster of yarrow, the wise woman's herb,

Its all-purpose magick adds strength to my words. (Toss in the yarrow.)

Petals of the red rose for passion and power,

Grant wisdom and love in this magickal hour. (Toss in the rose petals.)

Close the fire spell by saying:

For the good of all, with harm to none,

By fire and herbs, this spell is done.

FIERY HERBS FOR HEALING

For this fire spell's ingredients, check your spice rack—you may have these supplies already. Also, all of these herbal ingredients are associated with the element of fire.

Please be very careful if you are tossing in ground cloves. They are combustible. It makes a great effect, but when I experimented with this spell in my woodstove, my oldest son, Kraig, gave me seven kinds of grief about it.

"Jeez, Mom, what are you doing?" he demanded as I hunkered down before the fire with a teaspoonful of ground cloves in a measuring spoon.

"I'm experimenting," I answered him distractedly. I watched my little miniature fire, waiting for the flames to peak. "Okay," I announced, "here goes." I tossed the cloves into the flames and watched the *whoosh* of the dry herbs hitting the fire. The accompanying rush of flames, sparks, and scented smoke that billowed up the flu of the stove was most satisfying. "Cool," I announced.

"I can't believe you're sitting there playing with fire." Kraig frowned at me.

I looked over my shoulder at him with a grin. "Shouldn't you be heading off to class?"

"Will you behave yourself while I'm gone?" he asked me as he grabbed his backpack and began to walk to the door.

"Probably not," I grinned over at him. "I just wanted to see what would happen with a bit of ground cloves from my spice rack. I can hardly put this in a book if I haven't tried this out myself," I explained.

"Mom, I really don't want to come home from college this afternoon to find that you have blown yourself up experimenting with spells," he informed me as he started walking out the door.

"Oh, please." I rolled my eyes at his retreating back.

As much as it pains me to admit it, Kraig does have an excellent point. Be very careful when adding ground cloves into flames. I would recommend having them in a spoon so that you keep the spices off your fingers. I think using a small spoon is easier and safer, as it keeps the spices off your skin and you'll remember to keep your hands farther away from the flames.

For this fire spell you'll need:

* A cinnamon stick (for health and prosperity)

* A sprig of fresh rosemary or a pinch of the dried leaves (for purification and healing)

* A half teaspoon of ground cloves in a metal spoon, or three whole cloves
(for protection)

It is interesting to note that when cloves are burned as an incense their scent is
thought to drive away negativity and bad vibes. This spell also calls upon the Celtic goddess Brigid, the triple goddess of the hearth flame, family, and healing. Repeat the following charm, carefully adding an herb at the final repetition of each verse:

A fragrant cinnamon stick for health I'll feed into the flames.

Rosemary for protection and healing energy to gain.

Ground cloves do bring a flash and make the flames dance high.

Keep me healthy and strong, may Brigid hear my cry.

Close the spell with:

By the warmth of Brigid's fire, this spell is done.

As I will, so mote it be, and let it harm none.

Guard over your little spell-fire. Stay with it until the flames burn out. Make sure that
it is completely extinguished before you leave it. If this is an outdoor fire in a fire pit,
pour water on it if necessary to make sure that it is out. If you've built these fire spells in
the fireplace, make sure you close up the screen or glass doors when you're finished. Follow your usual fireplace safety and maintenance routine.

The ordinary arts we practice every day at home
are more important to the soul than
their simplicity might suggest.

THOMAS MOORE

Daily Magick for Hearth and Home

To close up this chapter on hearth magick, here is a daily magickal correspondence chart for your home. What makes this list different? It's geared toward the concerns and specific magickal workings for the home and family.

SUNDAY: work for success, healing, and blessings

Planetary influence: the sun

Household symbols: a rooster, a sun, gold jewelry

Colors: yellow and gold

Kitchen spices: cinnamon and orange peels

MONDAY: cast for matters concerning the home, emotions, and nurturing

Planetary influence: the moon

Household symbols: silver platters and bowls, moon shapes

Colors: white and silver

Kitchen spices: lemon rind and wintergreen

TUESDAY: a good day to work on problem solving, family squabbles,
and nosey neighbors

Planetary influence: Mars

Household symbols: a fire, black wrought-iron candleholders or an
iron cauldron or pot, red candles, dried chili peppers

Colors: red and black

Kitchen spices: allspice and chili pepper

WEDNESDAY: cast for communication matters and to improve good luck

Planetary influence: Mercury

Household symbols: phones, televisions, computers, letters, silver coins

Colors: orange or purple

Kitchen spices: dill and celery seed

THURSDAY: increase prosperity on this day; work toward expansion and
moving up in the world

Planetary influence: Jupiter

Household symbols: a dollar bill, coins, a paycheck stub, a picture of your home

Color: green and royal blue

Kitchen spices: sage and nutmeg

FRIDAY: cast for love, luxury, pleasure, and entertainment

Planetary influence: Venus

Household symbols: a seashell, a fountain, fresh flowers, your wedding ring or wedding photo, red or pink paper hearts, apples and cherries

Colors: pink and aqua green

Kitchen spices: thyme and sugar

SATURDAY: work for protection, boundaries, and house rules

Planetary influence: Saturn

Household symbols: a gate, a fence, a sprig of ivy from a houseplant

Colors: black or deep purple

Kitchen spices: Traditionally there are not many herbs associated with Saturn that are not poisonous. However, for banishing and the removal of negative situations, try a clove of garlic or dried minced onion.

Chapter Five

A *small house will hold as much*

happiness as a big one.

ANONYMOUS

SEASONAL, NATURAL DECORATIONS FOR THE MAGICKAL HOME

This chapter has four sections; each seasonal section is brimming with practical, magickal ideas for you to incorporate into your home and life. When you bring fresh, natural material into your home, keep an eye on it. When it starts to dry out or to fade, dispose of it neatly. Add it to a compost pile or put it in a yard-waste receptacle. Leaving dying foliage and flowers around the house doesn't encourage the kind of positive vibrations that you're trying to pull in, so keep your materials fresh and remove them when they fade.

No matter what season it happens to currently be, remember to take a good look at the natural world that surrounds you. Celebrate nature and bring a bit of its bounty into your home and life. There is always something magickal to be found in the great outdoors.

Many of the phenomena of winter are suggestive
of an inexpressible tenderness and fragile delicacy.
We are accustomed to hear this king described as a
rude and boisterous tyrant, but with the gentleness
of a lover he adorns the tresses of summer.

HENRY DAVID THOREAU

Winter Witchery

HOLLY

Holly is from the Old English words *holeg* and *holen*. It became popular at midwinter celebrations thanks to many magickal cultures and traditions throughout time. As one of the few plants that stayed luxuriant and green all year long, the holly, along with evergreens and ivy, became important symbols for the winter solstice. Holly was sacred to the god Saturn, a god of time and agriculture. The Romans first decorated with holly wreaths and greenery to celebrate Saturnalia, a seven-day-long feast and the big blowout for the Roman year. Schools were closed during this festival and the soldiers were given leave. Gifts were exchanged, and the mood was rowdy and fun. Holly wreaths and garlands were displayed prominently during this midwinter festival.

The holly also has ties to druidic lore because of it remaining green throughout the bleakest days of the winter months, and it has many ties to the faeries as well. It was thought that the faeries who lived in the holly bush came inside in the winter months to take a break from the cold temperatures and harsh conditions. (The branches and sprigs were thought to make excellent hiding places for the faeries of winter.)

In Arthurian legend, we have the tale of the green knight. The green knight arrived at Arthur's court at midwinter wielding a holly branch. The green knight was beheaded, but survived as a vivid symbol of resurrection. He was supposed to have calmly picked up his head and put it back on, while the court looked on in amazement. The holly he carried is a symbol for rebirth and everlasting life. This story also has ties to the ancient legend of the Green Man, another symbol of masculine and vegetative regeneration related to the evergreen holly.

The holly was sacred to the Teutonic goddess Holle, and the red berries represented drops of her blood. The holly bush is thought to guard you from lightning strikes and is generally a protective plant. So this year, place some branches or sprigs of fresh holly inside your home at midwinter and add a little old-fashioned magick. Check with a friend who has a holly shrub and gather a few sprigs to add to your household decorations. Here is a holly charm for you to use while you're busy "decking the halls." This would be a great natural accessory to add to your altar or hearthstone setup.

A HOLLY BERRY CHARM

Place three sprigs of fresh, berried holly around the base of a red pillar candle. Repeat the charm three times.

The holly is a plant full of magickal lore,

It brings protection and charm as in days of yore.

Now protect my home, bring us good cheer and holiday fun,

While we celebrate the return of the newly born sun.

Close the charm up with this:

By all the powers of the bright midwinter sun,

As I will, so mote it be, and let it harm none!

IVY

A pagan symbol for eternal life, ivy was banned from Christian midwinter celebrations as it was believed that when ivy was displayed, unrestrained drinking and feasting might take place. This last concern came from the ivy's links to Dionysus or Bacchus, the god of the vine. According to mythology, the ivy was named after a dancing girl who preformed for Dionysus. She performed so fervently that she died at his feet. The god was so moved by her passion that he placed her spirit into the ivy plant. From that time on, the plant bore her name.

Ivy is the feminine counterpoint to the masculine holly. Due to the embracing and clinging nature of ivy, it was labeled as being feminine (don't fuss at me—I didn't make it up!), while the holly plant, complete with its thorns, was considered masculine. Occasionally you will see this duo referred to as the Holly King and the Ivy Queen.

The evergreen ivy has become one of the more popular evergreens for midwinter celebrations. The ivy also brings protection, fidelity, and fertility into your home. Pick up a trailing ivy houseplant or a decorative ivy topiary and place it in your kitchen to add to your Yuletide festivities. Try repeating this charm as you add the ivy plant into your home:

> *The evergreen ivy brings protection and love,*
> *Ivy Queen, hear my call and answer from above.*
> *Bless my home with fidelity and joy, come what may,*
> *Grant us happiness and peace during the holidays.*

You may close this charm by saying:

> *By all the powers of green holly,*
> *As I will it, then so shall it be.*

THE YULE LOG

The word *Yule* comes from the old Norse word *jol*, representing the winter solstice celebration. It also is linked to the Saxon word *hweol*, meaning "wheel," similar to a German word meaning "the turning of the wheel" or "the rising of the sun wheel." The Yule log comes to us from the old Norse winter solstice celebrations. The Yule log is a symbol and a reminder of the importance of the power of fire. Its life-giving warmth and light were and are blessings to us during the darkest and bleakest days of the year. Also, fireplace magick performed with a Yule log would be doubly powerful. (Hint, hint: go back and look at the fire magick section in the last chapter. Does this give you any ideas?)

There are two kinds of Yule logs. One is a large log that is burned within the fireplace. Usually a small posy or arrangement of Yuletide greenery is tied to that fireplace log with a little decorative bow. The other type of Yule log would be a centerpiece. Typically this is a half log studded with three red candles and adorned with sprigs of fresh holly, pine, and ivy, with maybe a ribbon or a small bow threaded through the greenery.

Even though my family does have a wood-burning stove, we also use a Yule log centerpiece. We selected half of a white birch log from our woodpile and then my husband drilled out three holes for metal candle cups. Each year I switch out the taper candles and put in fresh ones after the candles burn down.

The candles are lit when my group gets together to celebrate the winter solstice in mid-December. (Since everyone has families, we shoot for as close as we can get to the solstice and a time when everyone can attend the celebration.) The taper candles are lit again on the actual night of the solstice, at Christmas Eve, and on Christmas Day, while we celebrate with our families. Finally the candles are lit again on New Year's Eve and New Year's Day.

Since the Yule log is on display for so long, I arrange silk holiday greenery around the candles and then add fresh sprigs of holly and evergreen on the day of the solstice. When the greenery dries out in a few days, usually right after December 25, I remove the dried-out pieces and simply leave the decorative silk greenery in its place.

YULE LOG LEGENDS AND LORE

* A Yule log for the fireplace should be kindled with a small piece of last year's log.

* A Yule log centerpiece should be burned for twelve days to encourage good luck.

* Arrange three red taper candles in your Yule log centerpiece to represent the Maiden, Mother, and the Crone or the spirit of the Lord, Lady, and the divine Sun child.

* It is said that those who attend a winter solstice celebration are protected from mishaps and misfortune for the following year.

* The Yule log has the power to protect the home from evil spirits and ghosts, and to ward off bad luck and arguments. (Save a small piece for this purpose.)

* After the Yule log is burned out, its ashes were spread across the fields to promote good crops in the coming year. Want to know why? This is also a handy gardening tip: adding some ash to your garden soil raises the pH level, making it more alkaline and less acidic.

PINECONES AND EVERGREENS

The evergreen tree is one of our most beloved symbols of the holiday season. Draped in sparkling lights and decorated with a dazzling array of ornaments, that decorated pine tree is near and dear to our hearts. Just as you'd imagine, the green branches and boughs were used to symbolize that life would indeed return to the land. Bringing evergreens into the home during the darkest days of the year was and is an act of sympathetic magick. (Plus it gave those winter faeries a warm place to hang out for a few days.) Draping fresh pine greenery inside your home or around your front door is a clever and subtle way to bring prosperity and healing energies into your home. Plus it's a joyous and natural way to decorate and celebrate the solstice and the magick of the Yuletide season.

Pinecones encourage fertility—those babies are loaded with seeds and they also make good fire starters for the outdoor fire pit, your indoor woodstove, or fireplace. Try gathering fallen pinecones this year and arrange several varieties into a pretty basket. (Gathering tip: if you have folks in your neighborhood with lots of pine or spruce trees, then ask them if you could gather some fallen cones. If not, check with a local park. If you ask first and only take what you need, they probably won't mind. Or pick up a bag of pinecones at the local arts and crafts store.) Enchant the pinecones for fertility and protection and place them on your table or beside your hearth during the winter months. Here is a winter charm to go with them.

A SPARKLING WINTER CHARM FOR THE HOME

Gather the following supplies:

* A small tube of iridescent glitter

* A basket (your choice on the color and style)

* A square of felt (to line the basket and help keep the glitter in its place)

* A dozen pinecones

Place the felt into the bottom of an attractive basket. Next, gather and arrange your pinecones in the felt-lined basket. Hold your hands over the pinecones and imagine the natural elements of earth, air, fire, and water swirling around you. Now picture this energy being funneled down into your hands and then sprinkle a bit of the iridescent glitter on top of the pinecones as you repeat this charm three times.

> *Pinecones are a natural symbol for fertility,*
> *I enchant these to bring us good luck and prosperity.*
> *By the winter winds that blow, and the sparkling snow that falls,*
> *I call for joy and abundance to come bless us, one and all.*

Place your basket on the hearth or use as a centerpiece this winter. Enjoy!

> *If spring came but once in a century, instead of*
> *once a year, or burst forth with the sound of an*
> *earthquake, and not in silence, what wonder*
> *and expectation there would be in all hearts*
> *to behold such a miraculous change!*
>
> HENRY WADSWORTH LONGFELLOW

Spring Sorcery

TULIPS AND DAFFODILS CHARM

Tulips and daffodils are synonymous with the spring. The tulip is aligned with the element of earth and is a very magickal flower. This bright blooming bulb promotes good luck and encourages prosperity. There are several different definitions for the tulip in the language of flowers. Each separate color has its own enchanting message. If you don't have a garden, pick up a pot of tulips and add them to your spring décor. They will bring a little springtime sorcery right into your hearth and home.

Just as with candle magick, you can match up the color of the tulip to your magickal intention. If you want to look a little deeper at the folklore of the tulip, the following magickal associations are based on the language of flowers. Try red tulips for love. Pastel pink encourages a dreamy romance. Yellow tulips encourage cheer and sunshine. White tulips signify a faraway love and encourage your love to return home. Deep burgundy and black tulips could be used to bring the magick of the night into your boudoir.

The daffodil was once called the chalice flower. It's not too hard to imagine how that name came to be, due to its cuplike center. Today, it is available to us in many varieties, sizes, colors (even peachy tones, white, and a yellowish-green), and shapes. The daffodil is associated with the element of water and in the language of flowers it symbolizes regards, gallantry, and admiration. Pick up a little pot of daffodils and place them in the center of your kitchen table or on your natural magick altar or workspace. They will bring happiness and joy into your home and add a little cheer to your days. If you care to enchant the flowers to bring some springtime cheer after the cold and dark days of winter, try this little flower charm.

> *A basket of tulips and a pot of daffodils,*
> *Bring to my home sunshine, cheer, and encourage good will.*
> *By the elements of earth and water, I bless these blooms,*
> *May their springtime energy spread into every room.*

Close the charm up with:

> *For the good of all, with harm to none,*
> *By earth and water, this charm is done!*

SPRING GREENERY

At this time of the year the branches of the trees and shrubs change every day. At first, in early spring, there is just a haze of color along those branches. As the weeks progress the buds burst open and blossoms and tender green leaves begin to appear. This season, try working with the earliest blossoms of spring for a little enchantment to add to your hearth and home.

The forsythia is synonymous with early spring. Those bright yellow blossoms are so cheering after the dreary days of late winter. Snip a few small branches of blooming forsythia and bring them into your home to encourage cheer and good-natured fellowship between yourself and all who live with you. Work a few blooming stems into a vase and set them in the heart of your magickal home, or where you have set up your altar or hearth stone. Here is a springtime charm to go along with them.

> *Bright forsythia blooms do encourage good cheer,*
> *May these blossoms bless our home and bring joy this year.*
> *Their energy radiates out from the heart of the home,*
> *Strengthened by the powers of water, wind, and the hearthstone.*

Close this spell up with:

> *From foundation to rooftop, this homey spell is cast,*
> *Elements four gather 'round, help my magick hold fast.*

BLOOMING BRANCHES

As long as we are on the subject of blooming trees and shrubs, be careful when you prune any blooming shrubbery. Take only the smallest amount that you'll need and don't go and raid the neighbor's shrubs or trees! Also, consider sitting next to the blooming tree or shrub and working a little improvisational magick right there and then. Perhaps gathering a branch isn't possible—then take only a few blossoms instead. Remember, if you take all of the clusters of blooms, there won't be any for anyone else to enjoy. Be a courteous and conscientious gatherer.

LOVELY LILACS

In *Garden Witchery* I gave the reader a few examples of the power of lilacs. The lilac is probably one of the most underappreciated magickal blooming shrubs around. They are sacred to the faery kingdom, the scent of the flowers encourages psychic abilities, and the scent has powerful cleansing properties in magickal aromatherapy. There are several colors available to us today—anywhere from white to rosy pink and many shades of soft purple. No matter what color they are, the stronger the scent, the better they will work for a cleansing. This spring when you start to contemplate spring cleaning, why not add a bit of natural magick to your task and do more than just vacuum and dust your home? Cleanse the house while you are at it.

All magickal practitioners need a good cleansing in their homes from time to time. Coordinate your efforts if possible to fall on the waning moon, for banishings. Or work on a Saturday evening to take advantage of the closing energies of the week and Saturn's energy for breaking negativity.

LILAC PROTECTION SPELL FOR THE HOME

Place a small vase of fresh lilac blossoms at the heart of your home. Perform all your mundane chores of sweeping and dusting, picking up and taking out the garbage. Once the house is set to rights, walk over and take a good whiff of those lilacs. Now ground and center, and repeat this charm three times.

The lovely lilac may be pink, white, or purple in hue,

Protection and cleanliness, their scent grants to me and you.

From the heart of my home, this power spins 'round and 'round,

No more negativity or anger can be found.

Close this spell up with:

For the good of all, with harm to none,

By blossom and scent, this spell is done!

When the flowers begin to fade, dispose of them neatly.

PANSIES

The pansy is a fun and readily available magickal flower to work with in the spring. This cold-hardy annual seems to be an ambassador of the season. On a practical note, the cheerful pansy is offered in a myriad of bright and bewitching color combinations. Match the color of the flower to your magickal intention, just as you would for candle magick. This flower is sacred to the god Eros/Cupid and is an awesome flower to work with to promote protection and love. Rumor has it that Cupid accidentally nailed a pansy with one of his arrows, which caused the flower to smile. Forever after the pansy's smiling face was shown to the world. Try chanting this flower fascination charm while you add these perky flowers into pots and containers for your porch, patio, deck, or home gardens this spring. Repeat this flower fascination three times.

The pansy's happy face is a blessing in the spring,

Protection, joy, and love this magick does bring.

Purple blooms for protection and bright yellow ones for cheer,

Blue shades for peace and health, red for the loved ones I hold so dear.

Eros, hear my call, add your loving magick to mine,

While I bless my home and family, come rain or shine.

The sun, the hearth of affection and life,

pours burning love on the delighted earth.

ARTHUR RIMBAUD

Midsummer Magick

The summer months often seem to be made for kicking back and relaxing. Well, unless you are a parent of school-aged children. Then you are probably running around like crazy. However, the garden is typically in full swing and there are many natural items available. Fresh fruit and flowers are in abundance and you should consider working with all that nature has to offer us at this time of the year.

STRAWBERRIES

Did you know that strawberries are sacred to the goddess Freya? They are a love food and are thought to ease the aches and pains associated with pregnancy. Wild strawberries are often found growing in your yard along the fence rows in an untrampled area. Make absolutely sure they haven't been sprayed by lawn chemicals before you eat wild strawberries. (Better safe than sorry.) Still, these flowers, foliage, and tiny fruits do come in handy as props for all sorts of homey spells and charms. The foliage of the strawberry plant symbolizes "perfection" in the language of flowers, so the foliage could be added to just about any summer spell that you want to turn out "perfect"!

If you have a friend who is expecting or are pregnant yourself, consider working with the fruits and foliage of the strawberry plant to bring love and contentment into your life and home. Pick up a package of strawberries from the market or go crazy and take yourself and your family berry picking early this summer. Now, if you happen to be allergic to the fruit of the strawberry, no worries—just substitute a favorite fresh berry that you can eat. How about raspberries? They fall under the planetary association of Venus, and they also have the same magickal correspondences of the strawberry.

A BERRY GOOD SPELL FOR LOVING VIBRATIONS

* A small bowl of edible berries

* A few strawberry leaves for perfection or a maple leaf arranged around the outside of the bowl (the maple leaf sweetens spells up)

* A red berry-scented candle

* A coordinating candleholder

* Matches or a lighter

Set this up on your altar, hearth, or hearthstone. Arrange the bowl and candle in its holder to your liking. Set the foliage down next to the bowl and away from the candle flame. This spell may be worked to safeguard a pregnancy or to improve your outlook on life by giving you a more cheerful view. (This spell also comes in handy when you have a walloping case of the blahs; adjust the fourth line as necessary). Light the candle and repeat this charm three times:

> *Ripe and fresh berries are a love-inducing fruit,*
> *They bring health and romance and happiness to boot!*
> *As I eat this berry, I now bring into me* (eat a berry)
> *Strength and love, well-being, and a safe pregnancy.*

Or use this line:

> *My strength, love, and happiness shine for all to see.*

Close up this spell by saying:

> *By all the powers of three times three,*
> *As I will it, then so must it be.*

Allow the candle to burn out. When it has, return the foliage to nature. You may eat the rest of the berries as a snack or have them for dessert with your family.

ROSES

Yup, roses are a very popular flower to work into spells, flower fascinations, and charms of all varieties. Working with the different colors of the rose is similar to working with candle color magick, as you may use the different colors of the rose for specific magickal needs.

Try white roses for purity and as an all-purpose flower; yellow roses bring sunshine and knowledge into your home. Red roses, as you'd imagine, are for love and passion. (Put those flowers in the bedroom.) Red and white blended roses encourage creativity and unity. Soft pink roses encourage gentle love and affection between family members.

Place a small vase of pink roses in a child's room (up and out of reach of small hands, of course). Or try bright pink roses in the main room of the home to symbolize the appreciation you have for your home and the people and animals who live there with you. Try orange roses for passion, vitality, and enthusiasm. Orange roses will also help encourage the movement of positive energy. Peach roses are for charm; ivory encourages steadfast romance between a mature couple and signifies the wisdom that comes with being on this planet for a while. Purple roses signify power, magick, and passion. Lastly, if you want to break negativity and work for protection, look for the darkest, deepest burgundy color that you can find.

The rose is also sacred to many goddesses throughout time and in many magickal cultures. Here are just a few:

APHRODITE: white and red five-petal roses

DIANA: dusky purple roses or wild roses

FLORA: all colors of roses

FREYA: full red roses

HECATE: a deep burgundy or chocolatey red rose (check with the florist, those dramatic rose colors are available)

LAKSHMI: yellow, white, and pink roses

LILITH: a deep burgundy thorny rose

MARY: all roses but especially white

OUR LADY OF GUADALUPE: red and pink roses

SELENE: a full white rose

TITANIA, THE FAERY QUEEN: all roses, the more fragrant the better

ALL-PURPOSE ROSE SPELL

When in doubt, try this summertime spell. It basically covers all the bases. Gather three fresh roses and a handful of fresh rose petals from the garden. (Match the color of the roses to your magickal intention.) Go to the heart of your home and slip the roses into a water-filled vase. Take a moment for yourself and calm your mind and heart. When you are ready, scatter the petals in a loose circle around yourself. Repeat the charm three times.

> *A circle of rose petals I cast by my own hand,*
> *Bring peace, health, and prosperity to where I now stand.*
> *I call for positive change, come in the best way for me,*
> *By my will and desire, and by the power of three.*

Close the spell with:

> *For the good of all, bringing harm to none,*
> *By flower and petal, this spell is done!*

SUMMER MAGICK FOR THE HOUSE FAERIES

Midsummer's eve is one of the biggest nights of the year for faery activity. If you have house faeries that you work with or if you want to encourage their benevolent presence on your property, then consider working this spell.

For this midsummer's spell you will need a vase of clean water, a few fresh roses, and some inexpensive, quartz crystal tumbled stones. Set the flowers in the vase in the heart of your home, altar, or at your hearthstone setup. Keep the crystals in your hand until the second line is finished. The time to work this spell is at sundown on the night of the summer solstice.

Midsummer is the time to work with the faery,

I call for your help, watch over my property.

(place the crystals by your hearth area)

I leave some gifts for you; do with them as you see best,

No pranks, just your kind assistance I do now request.

Close the spell up with:

In no way will this spell reverse,

or place upon this house any curse.

When you are finished, thank the house faeries in your own words and leave the crystals for them. Why? Rumor has it they enjoy sparkling things. It will also encourage them to leave your jewelry and keys alone.

The woods are full of fairies;

The sea is full of fish;

The trees are full of golden leaves;

Let's make an autumn wish.

ANONYMOUS

Autumn Enchantment

Adding a little autumn enchantment to your home and into your life is easy enough, especially when you look at this from a natural magick perspective. So, let's take a look at harvest and Halloween/Samhain natural decorations and items that we are already familiar with and add a touch of cottage witchery to these down-to-earth items.

APPLES

Apples are among the most magickal of fruits. According to many mythologies it is the food that grants eternal youth and immortality to the gods. To any mortal lucky enough to get a hold of a sacred apple, it was believed that consuming the apple would then gain them access to the underworld and bestow upon them the gift of prophecy.

When sliced crosswise, the apple reveals a star-shaped arrangement of seeds inside. This is sometimes referred to as the star of knowledge. The apple is a "secret" symbol for the Craft and is sometimes shown sliced crosswise on the tarot card The Empress. The traditional harvest and Halloween game of bobbing for apples may have some ties to old divination magick. As the apples float and bob along the surface of the water, people have to hold their breath, dunk their head in, and then try and grab an apple only using their teeth—sort of an ordeal by water. The point of this challenge or game was to test the petitioner. Going through water to get the apple was symbolic of the journey to Avalon (the land of apples). If they are successful, then they get to eat their apple, perhaps acquiring the ability of foresight and magick. Try it yourself this autumn. Fill up an old washtub with water and float a dozen apples in it. Let your family or circle mates take turns, and prepare to get soaked and to have fun!

If you are having a more restrained get-together, try hollowing out a space in the apple for a tealight and float these apple candles in a outdoor birdbath, fountain, or just a large cauldron full of water.

AUTUMN LEAVES

Here is a great idea that won't cost you a dime. Gather fall leaves and display them in an old jar or basket, or arrange them across a shelf or mantle with seasonal gourds and mini-pumpkins. You could also use these leaves as accessories in your magick. Try scarlet-brown oak leaves for knowledge and magick, and to invoke the wisdom of the Green Man. Red or yellow maple leaves sweeten up your life and may be added to charm bags to promote love. Add the luminous red leaves of the dogwood to any spells and charms designed to bring love and security, and to encourage a happy and protected home. Work with the soft yellow elm leaf for faery magick and for a glamour. Why an elm? Well, one of the folk names for the elm tree is elven. Or simply use the various colors of the leaves in color magick, just like you would a candle. Match up the color of the leaf to your magickal intention.

CORN STALKS AND ORNAMENTAL CORN

Porch posts wrapped in golden-brown corn stalks stylishly celebrate the harvest festivals as well as encourage prosperity and good luck. Corn is sacred to many an earth mother goddess, so think about that the next time you go to tie a bundle of these rustling stalks to your porch. Cornstalks displayed inside (or nowadays outside) of the home were thought to encourage fertility and to bring good luck. Plus it really sets the stage for a lavish harvest celebration.

Ornamental corn is a popular decorative accessory for the fall months. Often referred to as Indian corn, these brightly colored ears come in a rainbow of jewel tones and colors. Try stringing up ears of ornamental Indian corn into garlands that can be tied to the porch, above doorways, or across the mantle. Natural raffia would make a good choice for this, as it's fairly strong and the straw color blends in with the cornhusks. If creating swags and garlands with ornamental Indian corn just isn't your thing, then consider something a bit less complicated.

Typically ornamental corn is sold in bunches of three, which you could use to symbolize the three harvest festivals of Lammas, Mabon, and Samhain, or to represent the Maiden, the Mother, and the Crone. Hang a trio of corn on your front door or living room wall and enchant them for fertility, prosperity, and protection. Embellish these ears by tying a pretty fall-colored ribbon around their husks—that will jazz it up a little. Try out this autumn enchantment as you fasten the ears of corn up for display.

Chapter Six

The ideal of happiness has always taken
material form in the house, whether cottage or castle.
It stands for permanence and separation from the world.

SIMONE DE BEAUVOIR

OUTDOOR ROOMS AND THE MAGICK OF HOUSEPLANTS

PORCHES, DECKS, AND PATIOS

The porch, patio, or deck offers all the magick of nature plus the comforts of home just beyond your door. Here is a part of your home that is often ignored by the magickal practitioner. An outdoor room like a porch or a patio is an in-between place. It is exposed to the elements and the weather, yet it is still part of your home. And in-between places are traditionally powerful places for enchantment.

There are a few interesting magickal folklore tidbits that pop up from time to time concerning these outdoor rooms. The most prevalent that I discovered was the idea of painting your porch ceiling sky blue. Why? Well, to begin with, it is thought that it helps to keep flies off your food while you have a meal in your outdoor room. They supposedly become confused by the sky-blue ceiling and keep flying upward, to the false sky.

Also, a soft-blue painted ceiling is thought to keep away ghosts. In the old South, it was common for the porch ceilings to be painted blue. They were painted a special shade called "haint blue." And the word "haint" is most probably a slang word for "haunt."

If you have a large porch or patio, make it more inviting by adding some seating. This can be as simple or as elaborate as you care to make it. Check out local garage sales and flea markets. Look for metal or wicker furniture that is sound but that has some character—white and pale green distressed-looking finishes are wildly popular these days. You can always repaint the furniture or re-cover the cushions with fresh fabric. Watch for end-of-season sales and use your imagination. Look for small, charming bistro-style tables to accessorize your new treasures.

Even if a few folding lawn chairs and an overturned painted crate might be all your budget can allow for, it can still look attractive. Choose the colors with magickal intention and keep your outdoor room as clean and as inviting as possible. As weather permits, move a houseplant or two out on the porch or patio. Old canning jars with an inch or two of sand in their bottoms and studded with a white candle make for affordable and interesting evening outdoor lighting. Watch for garden lanterns and stylish citronella candles and set a enchanting mood with candlelight.

From a magickal perspective, decks are interesting places. They are typically several feet up in the air and may bring you closer to the trees and the wildlife that live in them. My thought on decks is that they are a terrific way to work with the element of air. Standing on an elevated deck is a way to give you a bird's-eye view on nature and on life in general. Working magick in mid-air, so to speak, is a wonderful way to put yourself in an in-between place—plus you get more of a chance to catch a breeze.

My parents have a large timber deck off the back of their home. Their property backs up to a wooded section and their deck keeps them up with the birds. Admitted wildlife fanatics, they feed the birds year-round at the bird feeders they have clamped to the deck railing or suspended from the trees that surround their deck. I shudder to think of the expense my dad has gone to trying to keep the squirrels out of the bird feeders. But the show the songbirds and wildlife puts on for them is always entertaining. They have had hawks in their backyard, several varieties of woodpeckers, and the occasional raccoon, which frightened my mom to death late one evening. Their deck is an extension of their great room; the drapes are usually flung wide open to enjoy the view, no matter what the weather. There is always something happening outside, and this way it brings a little of nature's magick into my parent's home year-round.

Porches, patios, and decks can expand our living space when you use them as outdoor rooms. Use these areas as a place to enjoy nature with all the comforts of home. Try dining alfresco some cool fall evening. Or fix yourself breakfast or lunch and sit outside during the spring, summer, and fall months and enjoy nature, the garden, and watching the birds. I do that all the time.

I usually take a break from writing around mid-morning, after the kids are off to school. I fix myself some scrambled eggs and toast, grab a glass of orange juice, and quietly slip out the back door with the cats as company. During the late spring and summer months the hummingbirds usually show up. They dive-bomb the cats or show off for me by hovering overhead and darting around to sample the red geraniums and the blue trailing lobelia that I always plant in hanging baskets and large clay pots on the back patio.

There is one male hummingbird in particular who is absolutely fearless. He has flown so close to my head that his wings often make my hair flutter back from my face. Once he zoomed in about six inches from my nose, and then stopped. He hovered in mid-air and then backed up to look me over. When I made no sudden moves, besides grinning like a fool, he circled around my head and then moved right over me to sample the flowers in the hanging baskets.

Now that we have gotten used to each other, this is our usual morning routine. I sit as still as I can and he delights me by showing off and proving just how territorial he can be. After he has checked me out, he zips back and forth between the climbing roses and the hanging baskets, chasing off any other birds that might want to check out the flowers for a snack. Occasionally this daring hummingbird gives the cats a thrill as he darts around. The cats hunker down on their bellies in the grass and watch him until he gets bored with us and zooms off. Then I finish eating breakfast and the cats strut around the back perennial gardens with their tails held high, as if they never were afraid of such a tiny bird in the first place.

The point of this story? My back patio is just a small area. Sure, I brighten up that concrete slab with pots and baskets of flowers, but it's not elaborate. The gas barbecue is there, and a hose reel for watering my gardens, and also four heavy white plastic lawn chairs and two little tables. It's simple and practical. We entertain on the patio, and I often meditate or work my herbal magick out there. The kids sometimes study on the patio or they sit there and talk on the phone. The whole family enjoys this outdoor room because it's a part of our house three seasons out of the year.

If you have a porch, patio, or deck and would like to bless the area and consecrate it into a magickal workspace, here is a quick blessing that ought to cover it.

AN OUTDOOR ROOM BLESSING

Clean the area, remove all clutter, and arrange the patio furniture to suit yourself. Gather together the following: a lighter or matches; one white pillar candle, for your fire representation; and a medium-sized terra-cotta saucer to place the pillar candle in. Collect a few pretty palm-sized stones from your property or some that are local to your area, and arrange these in a loose circle within the saucer and around the candle to represent the earth element. Add a fallen feather for the element of air, or use any incense that you find pleasurable. Finally you may use a small dish to hold water, or perhaps a seashell or two, for the water element. Basically what you're assembling is a portable, miniature altar. A good time to work this blessing for your in-between room would be at an in-between time, such as sunrise, noon, dusk, or midnight.

Arrange these accessories on top of a small side table or in the center of the floor. Sit down comfortably in front of the items and place your hands, palms up, on your lap. Take a moment and picture your outdoor room as one that pulses with light and magick. Imagine the four elements swirling around you in a beautiful multicolored ring. Once you've got that spinning away, take a deep breath and visualize that the circle of energy is seeping down around you and into the floor. Now take a deep breath in, and then let it out slowly. Open your eyes. Light the candle and say the following charm three times:

Goddess, hear my call and protect this outdoor room,

Elements four, bless this space and banish all gloom.

I call on the God for strength and for courage true,

Let me be both strong and fair in all that I do.

Close with this line:

By the powers of silver moon and shining sun,

As I will, so mote it be, and let it harm none.

Let the candle burn for an hour; just keep an eye on it. Now set your little saucer full of those natural representations of the elements in a prominent place, on top of a table or deck railing, where you can enjoy them in your outdoor room. As you pinch out the candle, say a spontaneous thank-you to the elements. Then, the next time you decide to stir up a little magick for hearth and home, you've got a little portable altar handy, plus your outdoor room is all ready to go.

Through the flower, I talk to the Infinite . . .
It is the invisible world. It is that small
voice that calls up the fairies.

GEORGE WASHINGTON CARVER

CONJURING UP A LITTLE
CONTAINER MAGICK

Now that you've consecrated your outdoor room, why don't we spruce it up with a few blooming plants? Working with pots and containers adds a bit more of nature's magick to your space. As mentioned earlier, red geraniums and red begonias are protective plants; you could always plant a few of these in a pot for your outdoor room. But we aren't limited only to those flowers. There are lots of options for hanging baskets and containers that will add a touch of herbal magick into your space. A good rule of thumb to follow with container gardens is to water them every day during the hot summer months. Plants in containers that are exposed to the elements can dry out quickly, so keep an eye on them. Also, when planting blooming annuals, remember that these flowers are heavy feeders—which means that they will perform best if given a dose of water-soluble fertilizer every other week.

CHOICES FOR SHADY SPOTS

If you have a shady spot, try looking for a blooming fuchsia in a hanging basket. This plant dislikes direct sunlight and will not tolerate any cold temperatures. The annual fuchsia's dangling blossoms burst open into ruffled blossoms in several shades of white, hot pink, and purple. As a hanging basket they are stunning, and they are also attractive to hummingbirds. They are readily available at nurseries and garden centers before Mother's Day. According to flower folklore, the fuchsia symbolizes a warning. So after you've hung up your blooming basket in a nice shady spot, you could enchant it for protection. Try this fuchsia fascination:

> *The fuchsia's pendant blooms are purple, hot pink, and white,*
> *With this charm you add security, both day and night.*
> *Your bold colors brighten up this outdoor room of mine,*
> *May your protection radiate out, come rain or shine.*

Another option for shady places are impatiens. Impatiens are the most popular annual shady bedding plants sold in the States today. They will bloom reliably for you up until frost. Some of their folk names include Busy Lizzy and Touch Me Not. The impatient may be used in charms and spells to speed things up. These energetic bloomers are wonderful in pots, hanging baskets, and containers, and they come in a wide variety of colors, such as red, orange, coral, pastel pink, hot pink, lavender, and white. There are also mixtures of colors such as orange and purple, pink and white, and a variety called the "peacock mix" that is white, soft coral, and pale purple. The markings of these particular impatiens remind me of pansies. Match up the color of the flower to your magickal intentions and spread a bit of energy and excitement into your life. Repeat this Busy Lizzy flower charm as you add these annual flowers to your outdoor room.

Impatiens or Busy Lizzies, call them what you will,
Add these flowers to your life and they'll give you a thrill.
Energy and speed they can add to my homespun charms,
As I work this magick with love and intend no harm.

CHOICES FOR SUNNY SPOTS

If your deck, patio, or porch gets a lot of sunshine, then consider annuals that enjoy the sun and hot conditions. Marigolds are a good choice. They are easy to care for, and the marigold is associated with the sun and has the magickal property of protection. For example, you could place the pot of marigolds by the entrance to your home to reinforce your wards. The scent of this flower helps to keep ghosts and negativity away. Are you being plagued by bad dreams and having trouble sleeping? Flower folklore says to scatter marigold petals under your bed. This will enforce a little protection and encourage prophetic dreams.

Marigolds are simple and charming little flowers. They lighten the heart and bring a little sunshine into your day. Pick up a six pack or two of annual marigolds this year and tuck them into a container. Think of all the wonderful magick they could add to your outdoor room. If you wish to enchant them for protection and to encourage happiness and joy, repeat this charm over the flowers.

> *Marigolds are flowers of the sun,*
>
> *Bringing joy, sunshine, and a little fun.*
>
> *Lady, hear my call, bless these blossoms so dear,*
>
> *As they help me to banish both dread and fear.*

Last but not least, here is a charm for those geraniums that I've been harping on for a while. I didn't want to leave you hanging by not including an all-purpose geranium charm to go with all the little tidbits of magickal information I've been slipping in throughout these chapters.

Geraniums will perform well for you in a semi-sunny spot. When the flower heads fade, follow the flower stem down to the leaves and pinch the entire bloom and stem off. This will encourage your geraniums to keep producing more flowers. Geraniums hang on through the hot summer months; as long as you keep them watered, they will actually bloom heavily again in the fall. (They love those cool nights.) Never underestimate this flower. It really packs a magickal punch. So without further ado . . .

> *The humble geranium is a Venus flower,*
>
> *It brings safety and a blast of magickal power.*
>
> *Red flowers for protection, white for fertility,*
>
> *Pink geraniums for love, coral for energy.*
>
> *Goddess, hear my call as I work this floral spell,*
>
> *Gently guide my hand and heart and all will be well.*

Flowers and foliage add a touch of nature's wonder into your outdoor rooms. No matter where you live, in the city or the suburbs, container magick is practical and simple.

Try working with the energies of plants in your home; you'll be amazed at what they have to teach you. If you happen to have a thing for indoor houseplants, you should really enjoy our next section.

A plant does not need to be rare in order to be magical.

DOREEN VALIENTE

HOUSEPLANT 101

Houseplants add their own special brand of natural magick to your home. Besides the fact that they are fabulous representations for the element of earth, they also add a healthy vibration to your home's atmosphere. For those of you who live in an apartment or do not have a space in which to grow a garden, creating a tiny green oasis indoors is the next best thing.

Most potted plants that are purchased commercially have been grown in a greenhouse setting, under prime conditions. Bringing a new plant home, into an environment designed for people, can be tough on your green friends sometimes. A good rule of thumb to follow is to read the care tags that are included with the plant. Just as with garden outdoor plants, how much light you have and how much natural light the plant requires may be two entirely different things. So plan ahead and buy the appropriate plant for the spot. And, since I am a gardener, let's go over some basic tips for houseplant care. (You can take the Witch out of the garden but never the garden out of the Witch!)

WATERING

Houseplants are most often killed or stressed by improper watering than by any other method. There is no perfect schedule for watering your plants. After all, the humidity, light, and temperature of your home fluctuates on a daily basis and changes during the different seasons. So how can you tell when is a good time to water? Stick your finger in the dirt! Push your index finger in to the second knuckle and see if the potting soil is dry or moist. If it's dry, then water it. Also, the surface of the soil changes color when it becomes dry. If you notice the soil cracking and pulling away from the edges of your pot, you've got a big problem. Those poor roots are dying of thirst—do give them a drink ASAP!

Tap water is fine for watering houseplants. The chlorine and fluorine that are typically added to city water won't harm the plants. It is not recommended to use water that has been run through a water softener, however, since the salt can build up in the soil of the plants. If you're really a purist, try using melted snow or collected rainwater. Plants may be watered from either the top or from the bottom. Use a watering can with a small spout, and try to keep the water off of the foliage as you water your houseplants. Wet the entire soil mass, slowly pouring the water in, until you begin to notice it seeping through the drainage hole in the bottom of the pot. Once that drainage stops, about an hour later, dump any water that remains in the saucer.

Watering your houseplants from the bottom pretty much guarantees a thorough soaking of the soil mass. Place the pot in a pan or deep saucer filled with water about an inch from the top. When the top of the soil becomes moist, the whole business should be wet. Remove the pot and allow it to drain. Then return it to the saucer.

Garden Witch Tip: Potted houseplants should always have a drainage hole. So look underneath the pot before you purchase it! If you leave houseplants in decorative pots without adequate drainage, your plants will start to develop "wet feet." Plants with wet feet start to look sick pretty quickly. Their leaves turn yellow or drop off, the flowers collapse, and those healthy white roots turn brown. Also, that stagnant water smells nasty. So make sure your houseplants have adequate drainage and half the battle will already be won.

LIGHTING

Improper lighting runs a close second as a frequent cause of failure with houseplants. Plants that are in proper lighting are better able to withstand fluctuations in temperature, high temperatures, and the low humidity that is common in many homes. And, as I mentioned before, know your light and check out the light requirement of your houseplant before you add them to your home. Here are some good tips for choosing a winning combination.

For flowering plants, you need moderately bright light. Plants that are kept in a poor light source will have spindly shoots, few flowers, and yellow foliage, not to mention the fact that poor flower color becomes an issue, as well as little or no new plant growth.

South-, east-, or west-facing windows are a good choice for most flowering potted plants, except for the African violet. (African violets prefer a northern window.) Moderately bright light does not mean a full blast of sunlight, however. Plants that are in bloom should be kept out of direct sunlight because the flowers will overheat and collapse more quickly. So pick your plant's sun exposure carefully.

Foliage plants are generally divided up into three categories: high light, moderate light, and low light. Try a north window so the plants can have daylight without direct sun. Or try sunlight that is filtered through a lightweight curtain for those moderate- to low-light plants. Plants that demand full sunlight ("high light") should be put in a southern-facing window. Also, keep in mind that suddenly moving a plant from one type of light location to another stresses it. Move your plants gradually. Ease them over into a new light exposure a little at a time. This is especially true with large houseplants. If the plants don't get time to slowly adjust, you may end up with bleached-out foliage or burnt leaves. And, finally, it is recommended that you turn your houseplants once a week to keep them from getting one-sided.

Last but not least, let's talk about fertilizing your plants. Brand-new houseplants don't require fertilizer for a few weeks. Typically they get dosed at the nursery or florist or wherever you purchased them from. For the rest of your green friends, try fertilizing these once a month. If you did this on the full moon, you could enchant the fertilizer and give your plants a magickal boost while you're at it.

Here is another tip. Don't waste your money on those plant stake fertilizers. Use instead a water-soluble fertilizer that is specifically made for houseplants. They are easy to use and readily available. Follow the directions and do not apply more fertilizer than what is called for. If you go overboard with the fertilizer, you can burn out your plants. If your plant is wilted, water it first. After it pops back up, then you can use the fertilizer.

So now that I've drilled some basic houseplant care into your head, let's take a look at the magick of houseplants. The following list will give you magickal information, planetary associations, deity correspondences, and basic care tips. There is also any toxicity information that I could dig up on these magickal houseplants.

In non-emergencies, try doing a little research on the Internet. One of the best websites for poisonous plant information is the North Carolina State University site. They have an alphabetical list of plants using both the common name and the botanical name. I actually have this bookmarked on my computer at home. The website is:

www.ces.ncsu.edu/depts/hort/consumer/poison/poison.htm

Another good website for information about plants that may be poisonous to pets and livestock is this one from Purdue University:

http://vet.purdue.edu/depts/addl/toxic/cover1.htm

If situations occur where poisoning concerns exist, then I recommend contacting a poison control hotline center right away. The free National Poison Control Hotline (for adults and children) is 1-800-222-1222. This number will automatically connect you to your local hotlines.

For pets, call your vet right away or try the National Animal Poison Control Center. This is the ASPCA and they do charge a fee. Their number is 1-888-426-4435.

Men are like plants—they never grow happily

unless they are well cultivated.

CHARLES-LOUIS DE SECONDAT

MONTESQUIEU

Magickal Houseplants

AFRICAN VIOLET: This popular blooming plant falls under the influence of the planet Venus. Its five petals make it a goddess flower and, as with most other purplish-blue flowers, it is sacred to Aphrodite/Venus. The violet is an excellent plant to add to faery charms and spells. The violet protects against faery mischief and promotes spirituality. *Care tip:* Always water your African violets from the bottom to help keep water off the leaves. If you fertilize your African violets with African violet fertilizer (this special type of fertilizer is typically high in phosphorus), they will bloom regularly. The African violet is nontoxic.

ALOE: The aloe vera or "burn plant" is a handy plant to have in the kitchen. The sap inside of the plant is great for soothing minor skin irritations such as insect bites, sunburn, and minor burns. This plant is aligned with the moon and is also used magickally for its protective properties. The aloe helps to ward the home from negativity and to help prevent accidents. This would be a great plant to work with in healing and protective spells. The aloe plant is described as having low toxicity if eaten and, according to the friendly folks at the Poison Control Hotline, has an "unwanted laxative effect." Also, some folks with extremely sensitive skin may develop contact dermatitis from the aloe gel (sap) inside the plant. This is usually mild and does not last long.

CACTI: These plants are ruled by Mars; they are protective and may be used to keep burglars out of your home. **Keep these spiny plants well out of reach of pets and children.** *Care tip:* These plants need high light intensities and are not suited for growing under artificial lights. Keep these babies exposed to direct sunlight and away from drafts and colder temperatures. Poison information will vary greatly, due to the vast array of cacti that are available.

CYCLAMEN: A popular blooming plant that is often given as a gift. The cyclamen corresponds to the planet of Venus and is sacred to the goddess Hecate. This plant may be worked into love and fertility spells. Placed in the bedroom, it encourages passion and fertility. Available in many colors, try the purple blooms for passion, the red for lust, and the white for fruitfulness. In the language of flowers, the cyclamen signifies voluptuousness. *Care tip:* Cyclamens will only bloom once. If you care to try and make it re-bloom, it needs to go through a long dormant period—not unlike a poinsettia—before it will re-bloom. The cyclamen is toxic if large quantities of the plant are eaten.

FERN: This plant has been popular since Victorian times and is a staple on Southern covered porches. There is something old-fashioned about hanging potted ferns on porches. The fern is aligned with the planet Mercury and is a faery favorite. The fronds of the fern are protective and boost the magickal significance of any fresh flower they are arranged with. The seeds from the fern were believed to grant the power of invisibility, and when the fronds are burned on an outdoor fire they are supposed to draw rain. Adding potted ferns to your outdoor room will encourage protection, good luck, and health. *Care tip:* Ferns are durable houseplants that tolerate low light but will perform better in medium light. Keep ferns cool and moist. If the leaves become brown-edged, then your ferns are telling you that they need more humidity—which takes the mystery right out of why they thrive on covered porches in the South. Some types of perennial ferns that are grown in outdoor gardens are actually edible. However, there are dozens of fern varieties to choose from; typically they are listed as having low toxicity levels. But better safe than sorry—find out the botanical name of your fern and double check.

FIG: The weeping fig (or, as it is more commonly known, the ficus tree) is a large and popular houseplant. Figs need filtered light and are happiest once they find a good growing spot to be left in that space. Turning them is important but moving a fig suddenly into a different light level will cause many of its leaves to drop. The fig was thought to guard against hunger and poverty and is associated with the planet Jupiter. The traditional fig tree is sacred to Isis, Juno, and Dionysus. This tree encourages fertility and safe travel.

IVY: The magickal properties of the ivy were listed in chapter 5. For those of you who don't want to look it up again, the protective ivy corresponds to the planet Saturn and is sacred to Dionysus and Bacchus. Care tip: The ivy is a good medium- to bright-light level houseplant. They need to stay well watered and prefer cool places. In the language of flowers the ivy signifies faithfulness and fertility. The berries of the common ivy *Hedera helix* (English ivy) are poisonous. The leaves are listed as toxic as well. This variety of ivy is typically grown outdoors. However, I would keep ivy leaves well away from curious, nibbling pets. A bite or two of an ivy leaf from a dog or cat shouldn't be an issue, but if they eat a good amount I would contact the vet.

ORCHIDS: Here's a tropical and romantic blooming plant to try. The orchid is associated with the planet Venus and is used in love charms and sachets. The roots of the orchid were also used for love spells. In flower folklore, the orchid symbolizes luxury and love, refinement and nobility; the *Phalaenopsis* orchid symbolizes an enchanted evening. Orchids can be tough to grow in the average home environment. *Care tip:* Mature plants need bright light for best growth and flowering. Plan on investing in a grow light for orchids. A few species of orchids do perform better in a home setting than others, such as the *Epidendrum, Paphiopedilum, Brassavola,* and *Phalaenopsis* species.

PALMS: The palm is a solar plant associated with the following deities: Apollo, Artemis, Hecate, and Isis. A fertility symbol, the palm—when grown as a houseplant—is thought to repel all unwanted astral nasties, spooks, and bad vibes. The palm is capable of putting off some very protective vibrations. Try placing one in a well-used room with medium light for best results. Palms grow very slowly indoors. Again, this poison information will vary widely, depending on the species. Many common varieties are nontoxic and a few have low toxicity levels.

PEACE LILY (SPATHIPHYLLUM): The peace lily is a popular houseplant. Work with this plant to encourage loving, comforting, and harmonious vibrations in the home. These plants adapt well to low light, but need medium light if you want them to flower. *Care tip:* Their white anthurium-looking flowers are long lasting. Keep the peace lily well watered and turn it to promote even growth. The peace lily is toxic if eaten, and if consumed in large quantities it can cause severe mouth pain and vomiting. Keep away from children and pets!

SPIDER PLANT: This easy-to-grow plant promotes protection. Try striped varieties to encourage boundaries and solid green varieties to encourage protection and healing. Great for hanging baskets, consider moving one out onto your patio, deck, or porch this summer. *Care tip:* These plants tolerate low light but will do their best in medium light situations. Keep these plants well watered and away from pets who like chewing on the dangling shoots. They are just too tempting to resist. The good news is that this plant is considered nontoxic.

There is so much in nature that can fill us,
day and night, through plants, animals
and flowers, with the eternal in life.

C. G. JUNG

GREEN MAGICK

I hope that this chapter inspires you to add a touch of greenery into your life and home. Now that you have all this natural magick spinning around in your mind, what will you do with it? I cannot stress to you how important it is to experiment and to try things out for yourself. If the plants you have weren't listed here, then why don't you have a little talk to your houseplants and see what kind of magick they would be willing to work with you? Many folks insist that talking to your plants encourages them to grow. Sit quietly, close your eyes, and place your hands on or just above the plant; see what ideas or information springs to your mind. The plant is alive, after all, so you will be able to sense a life force. That energy is a type of magick. Green magick is quiet but strong, and its possibilities are endless.

To close out this chapter, I thought I would slip in a houseplant charm. This is a great little spell to encourage plant growth and plant health. If you are giving a plant as a gift, try charming it first so that it grows well for the recipient. Have fun!

HOUSEPLANT CHARM

Hold your hands above the plant. Imagine a bright green and vibrant light swirling around it and then into the plant. Visualize the plant growing and blooming (if applicable) luxuriously. Repeat the charm three times.

The magick of nature is in everything,

Lavish growth and good health to this plant I now bring.

This green magick spell intends no harm or trouble,

It only brings pleasure and joy on the double!

Close the charm with:

For the good of all with harm to none,

By green leaf and stem, this spell is done!

Chapter Seven

Courage is the only magic worth having.

ERICA JONG

PROTECTION FOR THE HOME

I decided to start this last section off with the topic of protection for a very simple reason: one of the most common requests a magickal practitioner receives is typically an appeal for protection work for a home, family, or business.

The spells and charms featured in this specialty chapter are varied and eclectic. Most, if not all, are spun using natural magick techniques. While reading through this chapter you may be surprised by one section in particular: the conjuration of an astral dragon.

Now this topic may seem a little intense and out of character from a down-to-earth Witch who comes across as lighthearted and funny. However, protecting your home, property, and family isn't a job for the timid. Sometimes you have to fight fire with fire. But then again, the most laid-back, soft-spoken woman on the planet can transform into a tiger when her home, children, or family are threatened. Now, while I've never been accused of being soft-spoken (ahem), I have had folks be surprised by just how serious I can be. I do like to look at life from a humorous perspective; however, that doesn't mean I don't put my game face on when the situation calls for it.

So keep that in mind while you work your way through these specialty chapters. It takes valor and heart to defend yourself and your loved ones. It also takes brains and compassion to work defensive magick wisely. If you combine protective magick with passion, ethics, discipline, and courage, you'll make for a unstoppable combination.

If you have anything really valuable to contribute
to the world it will come through the expression of
your personality, that single spark of divinity
that sets you off and makes you different
from every other living creature.

BRUCE BARTON

PROTECTION SPELLS WITH PERSONALITY

Let's take an elemental look at a few ideas for protection, one that works with each of the four elements: air, fire, water, and earth. Perform these spells wherever you'd like—try your altar or hearthstone setup. Perhaps you'd prefer working at the kitchen table or on a dresser top in your room. Go with whatever works best for you. Look over these elemental spells and don't be bashful about adapting them to suit your specific needs. Adding your own flair to magick gives spells and charms personality and inherently makes them much more powerful.

Typically these protection charms and spells can be worked with simple supplies found around the home. For the dream catcher you may have to take a trip to an arts and crafts store for a small grapevine wreath or colored feathers.

AIR MAGICK

For protection magick that invokes the element of air, let's try working with a witchy spin on the dream catcher. Dream catchers are based on the idea that the web of fibers woven in the center of the hoop snare bad dreams and negativity at night. Once caught there, the bad vibes are held in place until the morning sun illuminates the catcher and then safely burns them out. The best place to hang a dream catcher is obviously above your bed. The next best spot would be in your bedroom window as close as you can get to the bed. Just make sure that you hang up the catcher in a sunny spot where the sunshine can illuminate it and burn off those nasty dreams and worries.

A DREAM CATCHER SPELL

To make a witchy dream catcher you'll need the following supplies:

* A small grapevine wreath (about four or six inches round)

* A spool of thin ⅛-inch yellow or white satin ribbon

* A few feathers (look for fallen feathers in the yard or purchase a small bag from an arts and crafts store)

* Beads of glass or semiprecious beads (look in the jewelry-making section of an arts and crafts store)

* A low-temperature glue gun and glue sticks

Start by weaving a pentagram inside of your little wreath. (Don't cut the ribbon at this point; work straight from the spool of ribbon. Only cut the ribbon after you've completed weaving the star and have tied it off.)

Secure the ribbon at the top of your wreath and tie a knot. Then weave the pentagram, adding a bead or two as you go along. You may want to knot the beads in place or glue them if necessary. Thread the ribbon through a vine or two as you create the points, to keep the star neat. Once you've gotten the shape you desire, use the glue gun and add a drop of glue at each point to secure the ribbon.

Tie on a few streamers at the bottom points of the pentagram and allow those to dangle down. Decorate those streamers with beads and a few feathers. To create a hanger, cut a twelve-inch piece of ribbon and thread it through the top section of the wreath. Tie a knot with the ends and you've got yourself a hanger. If you choose, you may glue a couple of feathers to the top of the dream catcher for decoration (see the illustration).

The trick to working with a dream catcher is that you have to empower or charge it. Once you've announced your intentions and have programmed the dream catcher, just hang it up in a bedroom window and let it do its magick. You will also need to recharge it from time to time. Try this charm to empower your new witchy dream catcher or to freshen up an older one.

Wrapped up in ribbon, this wreath is enchanted
Feathers for air, now may my wish be granted.
A magick catcher of dreams now creates serenity
Protect me from nightmares and ward off negativity.

Close the spell. As you hang up the dream catcher, say this closing line:

For the good of all, bringing harm to none,
By the element of air, this spell is done!

FIRE MAGICK

Okay, I admit it. I *love* candle spells. They are fun, dramatic, and one of those basic skills that every Witch begins working with. For this protection spell you will need a red, spicy-scented candle. The type of candle you use—a taper, a large pillar, a simple votive, or a practical tealight—is completely up to you. But there are a few things I have noticed over the years about different types of candles and the Witches who use them . . .

TAPER CANDLES: If you typically use taper candles for your spellwork, then you're a traditionalist. You probably have beautiful glass or metal candlesticks reserved just for magick. You are well-read and serious. This type of Witch likes structure, is intellectual, and prefers more formal rituals.

LARGE PILLAR CANDLES: If you primarily work candle magick with big pillar candles, you tend to work magick only when it's absolutely necessary—and then you go all out. This type of Witch can be moody and passionate, prefering to use one big candle for several days' worth of intense, heartfelt, and emotional magick.

SCENTED VOTIVE CANDLES: If you are into scented votive candles and work candle spells regularly with these, then you are sensual, creative, and down-to-earth. You like to do your own thing; spontaneity and improvisation are important to you.

TEALIGHT CANDLES: Last, but not least, if you are a tealight candle magick user, then you are a very sensible, thrifty, and no-nonsense type of Witch. Those fifty-packs of plain white, all-purpose, unscented candles just make you one happy caster. This type of Witch is a no-muss, no-fuss magickal practitioner, practical and thrifty.

And now that I've given you something to think about, let's get into a candle magick spell for protection.

A CANDLE SPELL FOR PROTECTION

For this spell you will need:

* A red, spicy-scented candle—your choice as to the shape and style

* A coordinating candleholder

* Lighter or matches

* A small piece of lava rock (from a nursery or hardware store)

* A picture or photo of your home, family, and pets

Work this candle spell on a Tuesday. This is a Mars day, associated with the element of fire. If the day happens to fall on a waning moon, then work for the removal of problems and the dissolution of danger. If you're working during a waxing moon, then work to pull safety and protection toward you.

Set up this spell with the candle in its holder in the center of your workspace. Place the photos of your home on the left side of the candle and the pictures of your family and pets on the right. Center the lava rock in front of the candle. Light the candle, making sure the photos fall within the circle of light cast by the candle. Repeat this charm three times:

> By the element of fire, I cast this protection spell
> Remove harm and danger, protect the home that I love so well.
> A simple lava rock adds magick to this fiery charm,
> Bring safety to my loved ones within the candlelight so warm.

Close the spell:

> For the good of all, causing harm to none,
> By fire's bright magick, this spell is done!

WATER MAGICK

In the opening chapters of this book we went over a house blessing and consecrating the magickal heart of the home. Now let's take this a step further and do a cleansing working with the element of water. Sometimes, no matter how diligent you've been, your house just feels "off." Maybe you've had the flu bug running rampant in your home, or perhaps there's simply a lot of negativity building up with quarrels and bickering kids. You'll know when it's time to cleanse the house.

Maybe a recent visitor or relative was carrying a lot of negativity and you feel they dumped it in your home. If you've had a run of bad luck or a rash of home repairs, it's time to start thinking about magickal defense. If the plants start to look crappy and no matter how hard you clean it still feels bad, then it's definitely time to do a cleansing.

This is a simple but powerful way to put things back on track. If you'd like to incorporate lunar energies into your magick, try this spell on the day of the new moon or the full moon. Don't want to wait? Then how about a Friday? This loving, Venus day would be a smart choice. If things feel really bad to you, then work enchantment on a Saturday and pull a little of Saturn's protective energy into the spell. Bottom line: go with your instincts and be creative.

A CLEANSING SPELL

For this cleansing spell you will need the following supplies:

* A bottle of spring water

* Sea salt—a teaspoon or two

* A bowl made out of natural materials (no plastic)

* A large decorative seashell (clamshell type)

* A small hand towel

* A silver paint pen

Pour the spring water into the bowl. Add the salt to the spring water. Stir the salt with your dominant hand—the one you write with—and stir the salt widdershins until it dissolves. Add the clamshell to the water. Now hold the bowl of water up and charge it with your magickal intentions. Say this line:

> *By the powers of water, this potion is blessed,*
> *Bring light and hope from north to south and east to west.*

Now start in the heart of your home and work outwards. Sprinkle a little water in the corner of each room. You don't have to soak the carpet, just a flick of the fingers will do. Also make sure you get all of the doorways and entrances. Dip your fingers in the blessed water and draw a star on every window, doorframe, and mirror. Once that is finished, return to the heart of your home and turn to face the west. Remove the shell from the water and dry it off thoroughly with the towel. Now draw the rune of protection, Algiz (ᛉ), on the inside of the shell with the silver paint pen. Take a moment to ground and center. Pick up the shell by the edges so as not to smudge the paint, then close this cleansing with this elemental protection charm:

> *See the silvery rune inside this seashell?*
>
> *When used like a talisman, all will be well.*
>
> *Algiz stands for protection, and it seals in power,*
>
> *From roof to foundation, and at every hour.*
>
> *By the powers of water, I cast out all harm,*
>
> *Bringing protection and peace with this simple charm.*

Add the seashell to your altar or hearthstone setup. Then close the spell by saying:

> *By all the power of river and sea,*
>
> *As I do will it, then so shall it be.*

Clean up the area. You may pour any remaining water down the sink. Leave the shell in a place where you'll see it every day. That shell is now a powerful protective talisman. Keep it on hand and incorporate it into other spells of your own design.

EARTH MAGICK

For our last elemental protection spell we are going to work with crystals. Now it is true that you already have your hearthstone or altar setup working for you. That has lots of earthy energy just perking right along. However, when working protection magick with the element of earth, we start talking about grounding and centering magick. What we are looking for here is to build you a solid, strong, and secure magickal foundation. Once you have that built, it's really tough for somebody else to come along and throw things off with random negativity or unbalanced personalities. So how do you ward them off? With strength, determination, and a strong magickal base. You achieve that by believing in yourself, by strengthening your own personal shield, and by beefing up your home's defenses.

TIGER'S-EYE SPELL

The tiger's-eye is an affordable and easy-to-find tumbled stone. It is a projective stone that imparts both courage and protection to its wearer. It was thought that soldiers once wore engraved tiger's-eye as a talisman for protection during battle. The tiger's-eye is a great tumbled stone to keep in your pocket to protect you from all sorts of mishaps and danger. It increases your energy flow and boosts your inner confidence and courage, which is just the thing for our upcoming spellwork.

For this spell, the supply list is short but sweet. What are you going to need? Yourself and four tumbled tiger's-eye stones. First things first: take yourself and the four tumbled stones and then go to the center of your home and sit on the floor. Get comfortable and close your eyes and focus on your breathing. Once you feel all centered and calm, open your eyes and set the four tiger's-eyes around you, one at each cardinal point or direction. (If you are not sure which direction is where, you can always place one stone in front of yourself, one in back, one on your right hand, and the last stone on your left.)

Now take a moment and visualize that you are surrounded by an earthy, warm, golden glow. Raise up your personal power as high as you can. (Picture your aura expanding out and becoming lush and full.) Now repeat the charm three times:

> *By the element of earth I work this homespun charm,*
>
> *Bring me focus and strength and cause others no harm.*
>
> *These four tiger's-eye stones cast protection around,*
>
> *Within these walls, no evil will ever be found.*

Sit there for a few moments and enjoy the stabilizing effects of the stones. Then gather up the crystals and place one in each of the farthest four corners of your home. After you've tucked the stones away, return to the center of the house and close the spell up with these lines:

> *From the four corners, I cast protection both strong and true,*
>
> *Lord and Lady, watch over my home and all that I do.*
>
> *By the hearth and home this warding charm is sung*
>
> *For the protection of all, with harm to none.*

O to be a dragon, a symbol of the power of Heaven . . .

MARIANNE MOORE

CONJURING A DRAGON TO WARD THE HOME

Well, I bet you're wondering what sort of situation would possibly make a Witch like me pull out all the stops for this type of heavy-duty magick? The type of situation was a masked stalker. Yeah, no kidding. A few summers ago we had a big problem in my neighborhood with some guy who got his kicks by skulking around and peeping in homes of teenage girls. He added a little terror to the mix by wearing a white Halloween mask.

It was the end of June when I first started to notice that something felt "off." At first it was a few weird dreams about someone trying to get in the windows, which would haunt me during the day. I said nothing about the dreams, which I chalked up to watching too many scary movies on television. Then things got a little more interesting.

As mentioned before, I enjoy sitting on my back patio in the evenings and watching the moonlight filter down onto the flowers. One mild summer evening while I was gathering a few blossoms in my backyard's perennial gardens for a spell, I felt all the hair rise up on the back of my neck. My stomach clenched and I felt a rush of adrenaline hit. I stood up slowly, armed with a pair of small pruning shears and a gathering basket, and looked around. I automatically tried to sense the yard to see what could account for the feeling of dread, but as I cast my feelings out, I only sensed that it was close. I stood there and silently argued with myself for a few moments. *I was a grown woman, this was my yard, I was just being silly . . .* and so on.

Unfortunately, the feeling of unease only increased. Deciding to investigate, I cautiously and quietly walked around to the side yard to the back patio area, trying to see what was causing the disturbance. I could see nothing to account for my discomfort. But as I made my way to the patio, my dread increased. For the first time in my life I was afraid of being outside in my own yard. I quietly backed up toward the door and eased my way inside. Once inside I checked on my teenagers, who were all sound asleep. Then I threw all of the locks and double-checked all of the windows.

Now that I was safely inside, my nervousness turned to anger. We have lived at our home for more than twenty years and I had never been frightened to be outside in my own yard at night before. What was up with that? I decided to cast a protection spell around the inside of the house and did so before I turned in for the night.

The next morning while I was getting ready for work my teenage daughter staggered into the bathroom to announce that she had been having bad dreams. "I think we need to recharge my dream catcher," she announced as she elbowed me out of the way to brush her teeth.

"What are you having nightmares about?" I asked her.

"About some guy climbing in my window," she spoke around her toothbrush.

"What?!" I demanded.

Once she was finished brushing her teeth, she told me about her dream. "So, can you recharge that thing or what?" she asked grumpily. I followed her into her bedroom to take another look at the purple dream catcher that was hanging above her bed from the curtain rod.

I stared at it thoughtfully for a moment. "Yeah, Kat. I certainly can," I told her. And while I was at it, I would put one hell of a protection spell on my daughter, I decided.

A week passed and all was quiet on the home front. However, I stopped any moonlight rambles in the garden. Every time I went outside, I felt intruded upon, that my gardens were no longer safe, and that my sanctuary was violated. I then began to notice in the daylight hours broken flower stalks in my rose garden and stomped flowers in the perennial beds, which I immediately asked my sons and husband about. Hmm, maybe things weren't so quiet after all. My husband and sons started watching the yard more closely.

The next week was the Fourth of July holiday. We did the usual things—watched my daughter's high school band march in the hometown parade, had a barbecue, went to see the fireworks. Later in the evening we were standing in the side yard lighting a few sparklers and watching the kids set off a few bottle rockets when I happened to see a person walking along the outside of our privacy fence.

I turned to my guest and said, "Do you see that?" We both watched as this person began knocking on the neighbor's windows. We have six-foot-tall fences and I could only see the person's face in the darkness but it did look odd. What . . . were they wearing a mask? I shouted over at the person as the kids inside the neighbor's house started to scream. The culprit turned, looked right at me, and then took off at a run. We looked around, but didn't see where he had gone off to. When the neighbor's kids started shouting insults out the windows, I decided to talk to their parents as soon as possible. Thinking it was just a teenage prank, I shrugged it off.

A bit later when the parents arrived home, I spoke to them about it. We didn't exactly get along. These were the kinds of neighbors you wouldn't wish on anybody. They had a problem with playing loud music at all hours of the day and night and the police department was always over there for one type of domestic violence problem or another. So I approached them carefully. When I mentioned the guy in the mask, the father went ballistic.

Seems this stalker had been hanging around their house for weeks. The father had even challenged the guy on the deck late one night with a baseball bat and the stalker charged him, knocked him down, and then jumped over my privacy fence and took off through my yard. (Which explained the broken flowers and trampled-on gardens.) According to my neighbor, the stalker kept coming back. He was using my gardens as cover and then cutting through our yard to get away. Because of the ongoing domestic problems next door, the neighbor hadn't warned any of his other neighbors, or even called the police to report the stalker. Idiot.

I thought about it all night. Well, that certainly explained the dreams, the fear, and the uneasy feelings I had whenever I was out in the gardens at night. First thing in the morning, I called the police department and told them about the problem. When the police suggested that I add more landscape lighting to the gardens and put the word out to the other families in the neighborhood, I got on the phone and started making a few phone calls.

That same day my husband and I added some more outdoor lighting to the perennial beds. This jerk's days of using my gardens as cover were over. Man, did he pick the wrong Witch's gardens to skulk around in! The longer I thought about it, the more annoyed I became. Enough was enough, I decided. So that evening I called a Witch friend for backup.

I called my friend Morgan, who is also a mother of three. She's a Reiki Master and one hell of a powerful Witch. I wanted someone mature, strong, and able to stand with me in case things went "bump in the night" while we were casting this big protection spell. Over the phone I brought her up to speed.

"Sure, I can help." Her voice came cheerfully over the line. "What do you have in mind?"

"I'm calling in the big guns," I admitted. "How would you feel about conjuring an astral being to ward the yard and the house?"

"How big are we talking?" Morgan wanted to know.

"Big," I answered her seriously. "Like in a couple of astral dragons."

"Jeez, you'll scare the hell out of the guy if he's stupid enough to come back in your gardens," she said, considering.

"That's the plan," I agreed. "The moon is waning so I think we're all set, astrologically speaking."

"Yeah, you're right . . . which goddess are we going to call on?" she asked.

"Hecate," I announced. "Why be subtle?"

"Excellent . . ." Morgan all but purred it. "I'm in. Let me get the kids settled in for the evening. I'll be there in two hours."

So a few hours later, Morgan and I set up on my back patio. The new landscape lighting helped to illuminate the shade gardens and was comforting and set a nice mood. What happened next surprised me. My oldest son, Kraig, quietly let himself out the backdoor, baseball bat casually swung over his shoulder. He raised an eyebrow at me, flashed a cocky grin, and then strolled over to have a seat in the shade gardens. From there he could keep an eye on Morgan and me and still see the entire yard. At six foot four, it's hard to imagine him blending into a night garden. But he settled in silently and kept watch on things. He became our sentinel.

Morgan and I blessed our working altar that was set up on the patio and then cast a circle. We called the quarters, lighting a large, coordinating-colored pillar candle at each point and invoking a different aspect of the Goddess at each direction. We also took a separate white pillar candle inscribed with a triple moon symbol, set that inside of a large iron cauldron, and charged that together.

By "charging" I mean that we both held the candle in our hands and then envisioned the goddess Hecate coming to our aid and that the stalker would be caught or leave and never return. We set that charged candle in the cauldron and lit it at the appropriate part of the ritual. What follows next is the ritual that we used. Look over this ritual before you start casting, as there are a few supplies that you will need.

A DRAGON PROTECTION RITUAL

* Consecrate the altar.

* Cast the circle.

* Light the illuminator candles and call each of the quarters in turn: "*Hail to the guardians of the watchtowers of the _____, I do call the element of _____. Lend your strength and magick to us this night. Hail and welcome!*"

* Light the triple goddess candle.

* Call to Hecate: "*Hecate, triple-faced guardian of Witches, hear our call. Turn and see the one who would spy upon our families and cause terror in our neighborhood. They cannot hide from your all-seeing gaze. Bring your focus on this stalker. May the stalker fall by their own actions, causing the web of fear that they have created to turn against them and to hold them tightly. Allow them no shelter, no haven, until they are apprehended and justice is served. Come forth, great Hecate, Goddess of the Crossroads and patroness of Witches, and bring justice. Assist your daughters and guard over those whom they seek to protect.*"

* Conjure an astral dragon:

> *I conjure a dragon outside of this circle of mine*
>
> *To bring justice true and to trip you up, come rain or shine.*
>
> *I conjure a dragon with sharp eyes and the breath of fire;*
>
> *Step on my property again and you'll feel more than my ire.*
>
> *I conjure a dragon to move silently and quick as a snake,*
>
> *You'll feel his breath on your neck and terror in his wake.*
>
> *I conjure a dragon to search for you both far and wide,*
>
> *No matter what mask you wear, you won't be able to hide.*
>
> *I conjure a dragon to haunt every move you make,*
>
> *Your days of stalking are over, and justice is your fate.*

* Take a moment and visualize the astral dragon. (Since I had a working partner for this ritual, we each envisioned a dragon. Mine was black, and Morgan's was red. We both silently reinforced what it was we wanted our dragon to do: to protect, to guard the neighborhood, and to scare the hell out of the stalker if he came back onto my property.)

* Release the dragon(s): "*Go now, my dragons of protection and power—find the stalker and help bring them to justice. Return to your native habitat when you have finished your task, harming no innocent along the way. Many thanks. Blessed be.*"

* Visualize the dragon(s) soaring off to do its duty.

* Thank the goddess Hecate for her assistance: "*Hecate, I offer my thanks for your assistance. I leave you this offering and my love. Hail and farewell.*" (Leave a small offering. Pour a bit of milk or wine on the ground, this works nicely.)

* Spin the circle widdershins, snuff the candles, and ground the protective energy into the yard or garden. Allow the triple goddess candle to burn out in a safe location.

* Clean up.

I guess you're probably wondering what happened next. That evening's ritual turned out quite nicely. I will admit that the wind picked up a bit when we called in the dragons, and then as we sent them off on their task it became very still in the garden. Later that evening, as I walked Morgan out to her car, baseball bat in hand, a police car pulled up. No, I assured him, I wasn't looking for a confrontation, I was only being careful. The officer let us know that they were increasing patrols as promised. He was very enthusiastic and sincere. But he did seem to want to reinforce the idea that the police would take care of things. As we waved goodbye to the nice policeman, Morgan started to chuckle.

"Um, Ellen . . ." she began. "Our pentacles were out."

I looked down—sure enough, Morgan's was glistening quite nicely against her black tank top and mine showed up really well against my black t-shirt. Then we both laughed even harder. Why? Well, my t-shirt had the word "Witch" emblazoned across it in hot pink letters.

The very next morning the police department called to let me know that the masked stalker had been spotted three or four blocks over from my home. This time several people saw him, chased him away, and called the police. Over the next few weeks the stalker had a tough time of it. Everywhere he went, somebody spotted him, the police chased him, or—oddly enough—somebody went after him with a baseball bat. (I guess the image of the baseball bat got sucked into the spell.) He never came back to my property or bothered the neighbors again. By the end of the summer, he had disappeared. A few months after that, the problematic neighbors moved out.

> *To live in right relation with his natural conditions*
> *is one of the first lessons that a wise farmer*
> *or any wise man learns.*
>
> LIBERTY HYDE BAILEY

BACKYARD MAGICK

For herbal items to include in your protection charms and spells, you may not have to look any farther than your own backyard. There are lots of protective plants available to you that are easy to find and probably right at hand.

Take a closer look at the trees in your neighborhood; for example, you could work with the foliage of the following trees: ash, birch, cedar, dogwood, elder, hazel, holly, juniper, linden, oak, pine, rowan (also known as the mountain ash), and, lastly, the willow. All of these trees have protective properties and a leaf or two (or needle) would be a fabulous addition to any protection spell that was listed in this chapter.

A DOGWOOD CHARM FOR PROTECTION

One of my favorite and easy-to-find magickal trees to work with is the dogwood. Not only does it have four-season interest in the garden, when it is planted in the yard it wards the property and the family who lives there. Try working with the blossoms in the spring, and the foliage in the summer and fall months.

Tie up a small bundle of fresh or fallen dogwood leaves—I'd say three leaves would work out nicely—or gather two small twigs (no longer than a few inches) and fashion these together into an equal-armed cross. Bind the twigs or leaves with red thread and hang it up inside your home. If you prefer, tuck it into an altar setup to boost the security of your household. (Please remember to be a courteous gatherer and harvest the smallest possible amount for your protective amulet.)

Here is a charm for enchanting the leaves or the twig protective amulet. You can work this charm on a Tuesday for problems with the neighbors and family squabbles, or on a Saturday for protection, no matter what the moon phase.

The dogwood is steeped in magickal tradition,
It grants wishes and bestows household protection.
Lord and Lady, bless this amulet, fill it with your power,
May my home be secure every day and during all hours.

Close the charm with:

> *By the hearth and home, this warding charm is sung,*
> *For the protection of all, with harm to none.*

A VIOLET FLOWER FASCINATION

For a little protective magick that incorporates flowers, try working with the violet. The violet pops up everywhere during the spring. Best of all, nobody cares if you pick a few purple flowers while you're out and about. The flowers and foliage of the violet will wilt quickly, so if you are planning on gathering some, take along a small cup of water. Sacred to the Faery kingdom, the violet comes in handy for all sorts of protective work. Gather three of the heart-shaped leaves and several flowers and tie them together with a deep purple ribbon. Slip the stems into a small glassful of fresh water and set this little bouquet up where you and your family or housemates can enjoy it. Enchant the violets with this charm to strengthen their natural protective qualities. Work this charm on any day during the spring months, during a waxing moon to increase your protection, or during the waning moon to push away negativity and problems.

> *Violets are a quiet little spring flower,*
> *They bestow protection, love, healing, and power.*
> *Long after the flowers fade, this fascination will last,*
> *Bound with a purple ribbon, this protective spell is cast.*

Close the flower fascination by saying:

For the good of all, with harm to none,
By leaf and flower, this spell is done!

Bibs, Bobs, and Whatnots

This last section of the chapter is designed to give you some ideas for magick using everyday items that you'll find around the house. Sometimes magickal accessories are much more simple than folks believe.

Here is an easy but powerful trick I picked up years ago while working the local psychic fairs. It's deceptively easy and very discreet. Back in the '80s they used to line all the psychics up at tables arranged end to end. There was one local psychic in particular that no one wanted to sit next to. This person was always crabby, complaining, and had a sour disposition. Unfortunately, if you ended up next to this psychic, you typically had few, if any, readings for the day . . . unless you went in loaded for bear.

Back in those days, the topic of Witchcraft was a no-no here at the Midwest psychic fairs. I was the exception to that rule because I never made any bones about being a Witch. I even lectured on the topic at the fairs. (Yeah, I know . . . I'm such a renegade.) But it was amusing to watch all the other psychics—none who would admit to practicing magick—break out all the protective crystals, candles, and incense if they were unfortunate enough to get stuck next to the crabby psychic.

As luck would have it, one of my favorite psychics, Mary, ended up next to the person in question. Mary was a hell of a gal—street smart, deceptively soft-spoken, and very talented. When I first started working the fairs she basically sponsored me. In other words, she kept an eye on me and if anyone had a problem with me or my Craft, they had to go through Mary first.

So there we sat, the crabby person on the end, Mary in the middle, and then me. Now Mary, she wasn't one for props. She just laid her cards out on the table and gave you a great reading. She traveled light and other than a tablecloth and a tape recorder, that was pretty much it.

Imagine my surprise when she came strolling in balancing three full glasses of water, a huge smile spread across her dusky face. She quietly set up the three cups equally spaced apart, across the end of her table, between herself and the grouch. Then she sat down, shuffled her cards, and grinned. After a moment, she beckoned me over and quietly explained what she was doing.

"Girl, you see those cups there?" she whispered to me.

"Yeah," I whispered back. "What, are you really thirsty or something?"

"Those cups there are making a fence," she explained. "They're gonna hold all the negativity you-know-who sends out and reflect it right back." At my chuckle, she wiggled her eyebrows at me. "You ain't the only one here who knows how to do magick."

And they worked—well, like a charm. Here's an easy protection spell and all you need are three glasses and some tap water.

A MAGICKAL FENCE SPELL

Take three glasses and fill them full of water. Arrange the glasses in a line between yourself and the problematic situation or neighbor. Think of this as a magickal fence of sorts. What the water does is collect all the negativity the other person is sending to you and reflects it back. There's just one catch—don't drink the water! (This is a nifty spell to do while you're at work, too.) When you're finished with the cups, pour the water down a toilet and flush. Run the glasses through the dishwasher or wash them by hand thoroughly. If you used plastic cups at work, dispose of them. Try this charm to go along with this simple spell:

> *Three cups of water make for a magickal fence,*
> *The water reflects, sends back and creates defense.*
> *A psychic's clever old trick that works like a charm,*
> *It teaches a good lesson but doesn't cause harm.*

A WITCH JAR FOR PROTECTION

Witch jars are quick, fun, and typically created with supplies found around the home. For this Witch jar, incorporating items that come from the house is a great way to link the protective magick for your home back into the spell. Look around and see what you can find to personalize this spell. Work this spell on the night of the full moon.

For this protective spell you'll need an old glass jar, like an old pickle jar or jelly jar. Wash the jar and lid out thoroughly and allow them to dry. Take a permanent black marker and draw a pentagram on top of the lid. Add to the jar several of the following items:

* A clove of garlic

* A few stray pet hairs (to add protection for your pets)

* A cobweb from your walls—I know if I check, I probably have a few cobwebs hanging around somewhere

* A few leaves from one of the trees in your yard or close to your property (check the list of protective trees listed earlier in this chapter)

* Old nails

* Straight pins

* Small bits of broken glass or a few colored marbles

* A small pebble or rock from the yard

* A straw from your household broom

* Sea salt or table salt

* The stub or drippings from an old protective spell candle

Finally, fill up the rest of the jar with dried beans, barley, and dried rice (to absorb any negativity that is lurking around your home). Now screw the lid onto the jar and give it a good shake. Hold the jar in both hands and enchant the Witch's protective jar with this charm:

This Witch's jar is filled with homey and simple things,
Now absorb anger and malice, rice, barley, and beans.
All negativity is drawn straight into this jar,
My household is protected with the seal of the star.

Keep the jar tucked away under the kitchen counter or in the corner of the most lived-in room. After a full lunar cycle has passed, at the next full moon, dispose of the jar in a garbage can off of your property. After you dump the jar, turn your back on it and walk away from the negativity. Don't look back. You are moving forward and on to bigger, better things.

Chapter Eight

Prosperity is not just having things.

It is the consciousness that attracts the things.

Prosperity is a way of living and thinking . . .

ERIC BUTTERWORTH

PROSPERITY FOR THE HOME

This specialty chapter focuses on prosperity magick for home and family with a natural magick twist. Now, many of us forget that prosperity is more than having lots of cash, it's more than having the most expensive clothes, the biggest house, or the fanciest car . . . actually, according to the dictionary that's perched above my desk, prosperity is defined as "the condition of being successful or thriving." See where we are going with this topic?

How are you thriving these days? Keeping your prosperity on track does include your place of residence. But tackling the issue of personal prosperity and abundance can be challenging at times. We all go through tough financial periods. The cars break down, sometimes all at once, our hours get cut at work, unexpected home repairs or bills hit us, and then we're scrambling. Been there, done that.

When things seem like they are overwhelming you, stop, ground, and center. Then put on your Witch's thinking cap and start working for both success and prosperity. It takes heart and determination to work toward improving your quality of life. However, if you're willing to work hard, and you combine that effort with magick, I have no doubt that you'll turn things around in a fabulous magickal style.

In this chapter we will cover many cottage witchery ideas for increasing the prosperous vibrations that emanate from your home. These positive and successful energies will influence yourself and the pets, roommates, or family members you live with.

To round up this prosperous topic, I'm including a few spells to help you sell your home, move to a better neighborhood, or find a new place to live. So, let's get started and see what sort of abundant magickal ideas we can come up with!

> *Ideas are, in truth, forces.*
> *Infinite, too, is the power of personality.*
> *A union of the two always makes history.*
>
> HENRY JAMES, JR.

PROSPERITY SPELLS WITH PERSONALITY

Crafting prosperity spells for your particular situation makes them more specialized, personal, and powerful. Do you really want to know what separates the novice Witch from the more advanced practitioner? They come up with their own ideas—and you can certainly do this as well. Start simple, and then add to your witchy repertoire. Check out the plants and colors associated with prosperity and see how you can adapt the following natural magick spells and charms. Live on the edge, change a few words around, and adjust the spells to suit your needs.

As before, these next four elemental spells are simple and easy to do. Try transforming and personalizing them by adding candles, herbs, or color magick, and discover for yourself what sort of individual enchantment you can add to cottage witchery.

AIR MAGICK

Maybe you only need a shifting in the winds of change. What better way to announce that positive and abundant change is on the way to your home than with the ringing of enchanted wind chimes? To start with, choose a small decorative wind chime for this prosperity spell. Perhaps you'll just enchant a favored wind chime that you already own. Celestial patterns, birds, or faeries would be a good choice. Metal or wood, fancy or plain—just go with whatever style of chimes you like. Find a tone that's pleasing to you and scout out a likely spot in your home to display them. Would the front porch work? How about the back patio, or outside a bedroom window? Display the chimes somewhere that you can see them and enjoy their music every day.

When you work this spell, try to hang up your witchy wind chimes on a nice breezy day. Once the chimes are in place, turn and face the east, the direction of the air element, and then enchant your home's new chimes with the following verse:

> *These magickal wind chimes will now ring out for me*
> *A homey charm for abundance and prosperity.*
> *Merrily do you announce the sweeping winds of change*
> *Banish poverty and dread, shut it out of range.*

continued . . .

Now ring in good cheer, wealth, and abundance so true,

Lord and Lady, please bless me in all that I do.

Wait until you hear the chimes ring out. Then close the spell with:

By all the powers of three time three,

As I will it, then so shall it be.

FIRE MAGICK

I have an "old reliable" candle magick spell to share. However, I will warn you that the prosperity comes to your household because you get to pick up more hours at your job. The money's not just going to drop out of the sky and into your lap. You are going to have to earn it—which is why my husband calls this the "Overtime Spell."

I like to work this spell on a Thursday, a Jupiter's day, to ensure that the monetary vibe gets rolling right along. You will need the following supplies:

* One fat green 3- to 4-inch-tall pillar candle (you may use a white pillar candle, if you prefer; it is an all-purpose color)—to add a little magickal aromatherapy, try a pine-scented green candle or a mint-scented white candle

* A cauldron or old deep pot for the candle to burn away safely in

* A nail or needle to engrave the prosperity and good fortune rune Fehu
  (F) and the dollar or pound sign (whatever the symbol for your currency
  is) on the sides of the candle

* A lighter or matches

* A spot to set the cauldron and candle where it can burn safely for a few
  days

Hold the candle in both hands and charge it with your intentions—in this case, prosperity and abundance. Set the candle in the bottom of the cauldron and light the candle. Repeat the charm three times:

> *By Jupiter's power, this abundance spell I cast,*
> *Increase my paycheck, send prosperity to me fast.*
> *I'm willing to work for the money I need,*
> *Please grant my request with all possible speed.*
> *This fire spell conveys no harm, for I have bills to pay,*
> *Send abundance to this house in the best possible way.*

Close up the spell with:

> *For the good of all, this magick harms none,*
> *By Jupiter's power, this spell is done.*

Allow the candle to burn until it is gone. This will take several days, so keep it inside of that cauldron or metal pot. If you have to leave the candle, put it somewhere safe to finish burning—try the inside of a empty fireplace, the bottom of your shower stall, or an empty kitchen sink. If you don't want to leave the candle burning, then snuff it out while you're gone and relight it as soon as you come back home. When your prosperity arrives, remember to give something back by making a charitable donation or volunteering in your community.

Water Magick

To promote success, abundance, and prosperity while working with the element of water, let's take a magickal look at the idea of traditional wishing wells. Sure, this is a no-brainer. You probably did this a bunch when you were a child: toss in the coin, close your eyes, and wish for good luck. However, before you go running amok and start throwing loose change into every fountain, fish pond, well, or body of water you come across, hang on a second. As someone who had to clean out all those coins people used to throw into the garden center's fish ponds and fountain displays—please don't do this!

Save your change. Tossing coins into a fish pond could hurt the fish. Plus somebody has to "fish" those coins out of there eventually, and it's a very nasty job. I can guarantee you they won't be wishing you well; they'll be swearing at your thoughtlessness instead. So, let's run—or should we say swim—with this idea and try thinking on more natural terms instead.

If you are at the edge of a natural body of water, such as a river, ocean, pond, or a lake, then try making your wish and tossing in a small pebble in place of the coin. Charge the pebble with your wishes for a happy and abundant life, then chuck in the pebble and say:

Spirits of the water, I give you a token,

Grant my sincere request as this spell is spoken.

Send prosperity homeward in a positive way,

May my life be rich and full, each and every day.

After you've spoken this charm, dip your fingers into the water and sprinkle a bit of the water onto the open palms of your hands. Consider yourself blessed by the element of water. Take a deep breath, smile, and head for home.

What I also like to do is use a green leaf to make my wish. Floating a small green leaf across the surface of the water is a better, more natural idea than tossing in coins, especially if you live in the city and only have access to a fountain. If there isn't any natural water source nearby, this is a good alternative. So choose your leaf to make the wish upon, hold it in your projective hand—that's the one you write with—and load the item with your wishes for success and prosperity. Now gently float the leaf across the surface of the water. As you do, repeat this prosperity charm:

> *A small leaf of green to represent prosperity,*
> *Float away on the water and send success to me.*
> *Water hear my call, bring waves of plenty to shore,*
> *Wealth and abundance will find its way to my door.*

After you've spoken the charm, dip your fingers in the water and rub it across the palms of your hands. Now take a deep breath, center yourself, and turn and walk confidently home.

EARTH MAGICK

One of my favorite cottage witchery techniques is creating charm bags. Charm bags can be a simple square of cloth gathered together and tied with a satin ribbon or you can be more elaborate and whip up the charm bag on the sewing machine. If you really want to get snazzy, you could pick up some of those sheer organza favor bags in the bridal section at most arts and craft stores and use those. They are a bit more expensive but they are available in a rainbow of sheer and metallic colors. For prosperity charm bags, I would select green in any of its various shades, silver, copper, or gold.

As to timing, either work on a Jupiter's day (Thursday) for prosperity, or try a Sunday, the day of the sun, for wealth and success. If you'd like to incorporate a touch of lunar energies into the spellwork, try working this spell on either the new moon phase or full moon phase.

The next step is deciding what sort of earthy and natural things you'd like to tuck into the charm bag to promote that prosperity you've been working for. Keep it simple and rummage around the house or in the yard for your supplies. This will also help to link the magick right back to your home. Add any of these items to your charm bag:

* A gold or silver coin (a gold dollar coin or silver dime works great)

* An acorn or an oak leaf

* Mint leaves

* A few whole cloves

* A cinnamon stick

* Tumbled stones (such as a quartz crystal for power, a malachite for cash, or an aventurine for good luck)

All of these natural items correspond with prosperity, wealth, and abundance, so choose your items and tuck them into the charm bag. Tie it closed and enchant the bag by saying this prosperity charm.

> *Gold and silver coins, crystals, and herbs of power,*
> *Lord and Lady, bless my magick in this hour.*
> *Bring success my way, as I will, so mote it be,*
> *May this earthy charm bag promote prosperity.*

Close the charm by saying:

> *By the strength of hearth and home this charm is sung,*
> *As I will, so mote it be, and let it harm none.*

Keep the charm bag with you, in your pocket or purse, for a month. You may recharge the items or return them to nature. Give the coins to someone less fortunate than yourself.

> *If I were asked to name the chief benefit of a house,*
> *I should say: the house shelters daydreaming.*
>
> GASTON BACHELARD

Whatever you can do or dream you can, begin it;
Boldness has genius, power, and magic in it.
JOHANN WOLFGANG VON GOETHE

EVERYDAY INSPIRATION:
CREATING A DREAM BOARD

Here is a dreamy idea for creating abundance and fulfilling dreams in your home. A dream board is a simple project that requires you to make a huge childlike mess with old magazines, catalogs, and scrapbooking supplies. It is a lot of fun.

You can do this in a couple of ways. Either fill up an old bulletin board with snippets of photos, quotes, and phrases of things that please you, or create a scrapbook page that you can hang up for inspiration, to remind you of the positive abundance and change you are pulling into your life.

For example, when I started this book, I was smack dab in the middle of another manuscript, which just wasn't going where I wanted it to. I spent a good four months in frustration trying to get it up and moving, all to no avail. Then one day I was thumbing through a gardening magazine, trying to find some inspiration, when I came across a wonderful photo of a cottage surrounded by gardens. The photo spread had a romantic, old-fashioned, magickal look about it. I sighed over the photos for a time, and then tore out my favorite picture.

I went back to my computer for one more shot at the stalled book project and tacked the picture to my bulletin board that hangs behind my computer. I said a quick prayer to the Goddess, asking her to send me some insight and inspiration so I could get that manuscript moving. I prayed for success and for prosperity, and for enthusiasm on the stalled topic, so I could create a fun and clever manuscript that my editors would be enthusiastic about. Confident in my prayers, I smiled and told myself to be a professional and get back to work. So did I just whip out the rest of that troublesome manuscript? Nope, something else happened instead. Something magickal . . .

Those romantic, cottage-filled pictures kept popping up in my mind. I found myself just sitting at the bulletin board and daydreaming about the idea of a Witch's cottage. Before you knew it, I had opened a new file on my desktop and started working out a rough outline. I blinked at it, then saved it under "cottage" and told myself to get back to work—thinking that if I put the cottage ideas down, I could then put it aside. *Wrong.*

Hello, synchronicity! Every time I turned around, the word "cottage" jumped out at me. I started dreaming about chapter ideas for a book about a Witch's house. The little notebook I always carry with me became full of quotes, thoughts, and ideas for a book about home magick. I started a folder filled with ideas and kept adding to that bulletin board.

I eventually got so distracted by the rapid-fire ideas for a cottage book that while driving the car I would use traffic lights as stop signs. My kids threatened to make me pull over so they could drive. (Jeez, that only happened once. There weren't any oncoming cars or anything. Can't a person claim artistic distraction?)

Finally I gave in. I had asked for inspiration, after all. Why didn't I just follow this tug at my heart and see where it led me? A few days later, I tucked the stalled manuscript away in a folder and loaded that bulletin board with more cottagey photos, snippets of hearth and home quotes, and illustrations that made me smile. Then I put together a more defined outline for *Cottage Witchery* and called my editor. What do you know? She liked the idea.

I was off and running. A few months later, I turned in a proposal and it was contracted quickly. So, yeah, I absolutely believe in the power of creating a magickal dream board for success. If I didn't, you wouldn't be reading this book right now.

Here's what you will need:

* A bulletin board and push pins, or a blank, heavyweight scrapbook page and page protector

* Glue stick

* Scissors

* Scraps of decorative papers

* Old magazines, catalogs, and photos of whatever you're dreaming about

This is the fun part. Remember when you were a kid and they turned you loose in school to make a collage? Well, here you go. Be prepared to make a huge mess. But honestly, that's half the fun. If you are into scrapbooking, drag out those supplies and stickers and see what you can craft.

If this board is geared toward starting a family, or adopting a new member into yours, then fill it full of baby pictures and quotes about children, home, and family. If you're waiting to adopt, then try adding photos of children from all over the world to those family-oriented snippets and quotes.

Perhaps you want to inspire yourself to try for a promotion or land that "dream job." Well, what images and words make you dream of your perfect job or career? Let's say you want to save up for a vacation. Well, then, find a picture of the location you wish to go and make that your theme. Start a savings account and keep that board in a spot where you'll be reminded to keep saving up for that dream vacation. Are you looking to re-model the kitchen or redo the bathroom in your house? Pick up a few home improvement magazines and pull out the photos and ideas that really appeal to you. Add a few paint chips and make the board into a wish list/renovation idea board. The possibilities are endless.

Once you have all the components arranged, hold the board or page in your hands and enchant it for success, using this charm:

> *Snippets of paper, photos, scissors, and glue,*
>
> *Following your heart's dream is easy to do,*
>
> *I enchant this dream board for luck and success,*
>
> *As I work toward my goals, I will be blessed.*
>
> *Filled with happy images that I am pulling my way,*
>
> *Prosperity and success are the order of the day.*

Hang up your dream board someplace in your home where you'll see it and be inspired every day. Start taking steps toward fulfilling those dreams and see where this positive path leads you.

When you have too much month for your paycheck,

then what you need to do is realize that

there is abundance all around you and

focus on the abundance and not your lack . . .

as night follows day, abundance will come to you.

SIDNEY MADWED

BACKYARD MAGICK

Do you know what the best part about working prosperity magick for hearth and home with natural supplies is? It rarely costs you anything. There is a plethora of plants and trees out there that are aligned with prosperity, abundance, and wealth. You can find them growing all around you! Go take a walk and see what magickal plant materials nature has to offer. Look for these trees: ash, cedar, elder, oak, pine, and the poplar. See if you can pick up a fallen twig, leaf, pinecone, or acorn to work with.

An oak tree planted in the yard is a type of marker. This denotes a magickal property; the oak tree is well liked by nature spirits and faeries. Associated with many sky gods, including Jupiter, Zeus, and Thor, this tree also symbolizes the Oak King, the god of the waxing year. The noble oak is also one of the trees sacred to the hearth goddess Brigid. It has the elemental association of the element of fire, and working with the foliage or fruit (the acorns) will bring success, distinction, wealth, and prosperity to your home.

AN OAK SPELL FOR PROSPERITY AND ABUNDANCE

Gather the following:

* Three acorns or oak leaves

* A small piece of paper

* A green ink pen or marker

* A tealight

* A tealight holder

* Matches or a lighter

Work this spell on a Thursday for prosperity or a Sunday for wealth and success. As before, those moon phases that are the most opportune are the waxing moon and the full moon. Gather three fallen acorns or three oak leaves. Take a small piece of paper with your name and address written on it with the green pen. Fold the slip of paper into thirds and tuck it in the bottom of the tealight candle's metal cup. Replace the candle into its cup and place it inside the candleholder. Arrange these items on your natural magick workspace or your hearthstone setup. Light the candle and repeat the following charm three times:

The oak tree is full of strength, magick, and power,

Brigid, hear my call in this enchanted hour.

Bring my house prosperity with the charm I rhyme,

This spell will create abundance, come rain or shine.

By all the magick of leaf and tree,

As I do will it, so shall it be.

After the tealight candle burns out, the slip of paper will be covered in wax and sealed in the bottom of the cup. The spell is safely sealed; you may dispose of the metal cup. Return the leaves and acorns to nature as an offering.

A HONEYSUCKLE FLOWER FASCINATION

The flowering honeysuckle vine or shrub brings prosperity when grown on your property, making it a great plant to incorporate into any prosperity spell. For this flower fascination, you are creating a representation of each of the four elements. The plants represent the element of earth. The scent of the flowers symbolizes air. The candle flames are for fire and the water in the vase obviously takes care of the element of water.

For starters, I would tuck the honeysuckle stems and leaves in a vase of fresh water. Alternatively, if you gathered a honeysuckle blossom or two, then float it in a glass or small bowl of water. Circle the four candles with loose honeysuckle leaves. Flower folklore tells us that this is a way to attract money to your home. Light one of the candles at the end of each line of the charm.

Work a flower fascination with the elements four,

Green candles in a ring call prosperity to our door.

A sweet and charming scent has the honeysuckle bloom,

Its flower magick spreads wealth into every room.

Raise your energy up as high as you can. Place your hands on the work surface. Visualize the prosperity and abundance arriving to your door in the best way for you. Then close the spell with:

For the good of all, bringing harm to none,

By flower and color, this spell is done.

Allow the candles to burn out. Keep the honeysuckle in the home until it begins to fade, then neatly return it to nature.

Why scurry about looking for the truth?

. . . Can you be still and see it in the mountain?

The pine tree? yourself?

LOA-TZU

PLANTS FOR PROSPERITY MAGICK

Here is a quick listing of ten additional backyard plants you can incorporate into your prosperity and abundance spells and charms for hearth and home. (Some of these backyard plants also have protective properties.)

Following the list is a simple worksheet for natural magick. Work out the charms and spells on this worksheet that you would enjoy performing for hearth and home. If you need to double-check which days of the week are most opportune for certain types of magick, flip back to the end of chapter 4. Bottom line: don't be afraid to improvise. Put your heart into it, get creative, and have fun.

BERGAMOT (BEE BALM): Corresponds to Mercury and the element of air. Slip the scented leaves into charm bags or tuck them into your wallet to draw money. This popular garden plant grows well in sun or part shade.

CHAMOMILE: Corresponds to the Sun and the element of water. Add a few dainty chamomile blossoms to any spell for prosperity and for household protection.

CLOVER (with three or four leaves): Corresponds to Mercury and aligns to the element of air. Three-leaf clovers represent the goddess Brigid and the triple goddess. Four-leaf clovers are traditionally for good luck and prosperity charms.

FERNS: Corresponds to Mercury and aligns to the element of air. Carrying a fern frond was thought to bring prosperity and good luck. Adding fern foliage to a vase of fresh flowers increases their magickal properties and bestows luck and protection on the home.

HELIOTROPE: Aligns with the Sun and the element of fire. Place the dusky, cherry-scented blossoms in your pocket to draw riches.

JASMINE: Links to the Moon and the element of water. This is a feminine plant suitable for any lunar magick. Carrying or wearing jasmine flowers is a sure way to draw riches and prosperity into your life.

PERIWINKLE OR SORCERER'S VIOLET (also known as "vinca minor"): This shade-loving groundcover is often overlooked as a magickal plant. This is a very popular plant in the nursery trade, so check out the groundcover section and add some of this to the shady spots on your property. Periwinkle aligns to the planet Venus and the element of water. Tuck a snippet of the blooming vine in your pocket to draw money. The periwinkle can also be used for bindings, protection, and love.

SWEET WOODRUFF: Another shade-loving groundcover. This plant is linked to the planet Mars and the element of fire. Carried, the plant attracts money and is a protective talisman for athletes. (Have them place it in their duffle bag holding their sports equipment.) This plant also promotes victory.

TOMATO: Corresponds with the planet Venus and the element of water. Believe it or not, the tomato pulls in prosperity when grown on your property. Try growing a patio tomato in a container on your sunny porch, patio, or deck this year. The tomato is also a protective plant, so it will reinforce protective wards in your outdoor rooms. When consumed, the tomato encourages loving feelings, which may explain the old folk name for the tomato, the "love apple."

TULIP: The tulip is connected to the planet Venus and the element of earth. When grown in the yard, the tulip encourages the home to have a prosperous atmosphere. It is used to ward off poverty and bad luck in general.

Natural Magick Worksheet

GOAL: _____

_____

_____

DAY: _____

_____

_____

MOON PHASE: _____

_____

_____

MAGICKAL PLANT(S) OR HERB USED: _____

_____

_____

CANDLE COLOR: _____

_____

_____

CRYSTALS OR STONES: _____

_____

_____

CHARM OR VERSE: _____

_____

_____

Much effort, much prosperity.

EURIPIDES

MOVING ON UP:
MAGICK FOR SELLING OR BUYING A HOME

No doubt about it, working for prosperity and abundance is a lot of work. But you definitely get out of it whatever you put into it. It's sort of like that old Wiccan joke about the newbie who is disappointed that the spell they did to get a great job didn't pan out as they intended. The novice is completely mystified until they find out that they actually had to go out and apply, and then interview, for that job.

The same idea goes with this prosperity chapter; the money isn't going to just go *poof* and then appear out of thin air. You'll have to do something extra and put some effort into it. So, obviously, if you are after a better job or more pay, then be willing to work for it and follow it up with a magickal plan. Combining prosperity magick with common sense and hard work is an unbeatable combination—so get in there and go for it!

We are going to close up this chapter with a spell to assist with the selling of your home and another for finding a new home. First things first, if you're in the market to sell, find a reputable real estate person and ask for a fair price. Be honest when you talk to the realtor about your home and any problems there may be after the inspection. If you are going to use magick, then be honest and don't magickally camouflage any problems—because if you go casting a glamour to hide the problems, chances are when you move into your new home even more hidden problems will be waiting for you. Karma will find you, on that you can depend.

The best thing to do is to do a big cleansing when you put the house on the market. Making the atmosphere welcoming to those prospective buyers will help you out in the long run. (Take another look at chapters 1 and 2 for ideas.) Once the house has a great welcoming vibration going, then work the following charm to help attract potential buyers.

HOUSE-SELLING CHARM

Gather together the ad for your house, the key to the front door (or whatever key you are giving to the realtor) and, lastly, a white candle in a coordinating holder. You can work this charm during a waxing moon phase or at the new or full moon. Arrange the candle on top of the ad for your home and place the key in front of the candle. Light the candle and repeat the charm three times. When you are finished, allow the candle to burn out on its own.

> *Elements four, gather 'round to the sound of my voice,*
> *We desire to move up in the world, this is our choice.*
> *The house is a good one, from attic to basement stairs,*
> *Help our house to sell quickly and at a price that's fair.*
> *From rooftop to foundation, this homey charm is cast,*
> *Send us a willing buyer and make my magick last.*

HOUSE-BUYING CHARM

If you've found the home of your dreams and you are putting in a bid, try this charm to help improve your chances of getting that house. Work this spell at the full moon phase, if possible, or on a Monday for its lunar energies.

For this spell you will need a representation of the moon goddess—a drawing or a white rose in a vase will suffice. You will also need a small tumbled moonstone, a white or silver candle, and a photo of the house that you have bid on.

Take the photo or the ad for the house outside, under the light of the moon. Hold the picture out in the palms of your hands. Let the moonlight fall across this for a few moments. Now take the picture inside and set it up on your hearthstone or natural magick altar. Put any other papers up there that have to do with the offer that you have made on the property. Set the goddess representation on top of the papers. Add that moonstone to the stack for moon magick and to reinforce that you'd like to move to a new location. (Moonstones traditionally are used for safe travel and lunar magick.) Light the candle and repeat the following charm:

> *I have found the perfect house of my dreams,*
> *Send my wish out on a silver moonbeam.*
> *Sell this house to me and I will care for it well,*
> *Goddess, hear my request and assist in this spell.*

Close the spell by saying:

> *Thank you, Goddess, for your love, magick, and care,*
> *I close this spell by earth, water, fire, and air.*

BIBS, BOBS, AND WHATNOTS

A young Witch friend of mine suggested this next practical magickal working. It won't cost you a dime and is fun to do, to boot! Have you ever built a cairn? A cairn is an arrangement of rocks, typically in a pyramidal or triangular shape, that is used in magick to physically represent a spell or a goal that you are trying to reach. This stack of rocks actually represents the astral energy that you are building up while you work toward that goal. In this case, we will be building up your prosperity. By using rocks from your surrounding area, you link the magick back to the earth that your home stands on. All those great elemental energies associated with the earth, such as fertility, abundance, and prosperity, are just waiting to be tapped into.

All you need to perform this spell is about a dozen or so small- to palm-sized rocks from your property. If you live in an apartment complex, then gather the stones from the area around your building. To set the cairn up, you will need a small area that can remain undisturbed. So scout out a spot in the yard or even on your patio or porch and begin stacking up those rocks.

Concentrate on your goal while you are gathering the stones and as you build the cairn. With every rock, you are adding more intention and energy into this prosperity spell. As you build up the shape of stones, say the following verse to link your magick to your goal:

I build this cairn for prosperity,
Bring success, abundance, and wealth to me.
By the element of earth, this spell is cast,
May my fortune increase and my pleasure last.

Leave the cairn undisturbed for at least a full moon cycle (twenty-eight days). You may refresh the spell by repeating the charm and tidying up the cairn every month.

Want a few more ideas? Take a look at what things you have lying around the house; what do you suppose you could do with them to create a little prosperity? Got any old glass jars? You can make a Witch's jar for prosperity and set it out on the counter. Every time you find any loose change, put it in the jar. Paint the lid of the jar green and draw the prosperity rune Fehu (ᚠ) on the top.

Try empowering a bundle of cinnamon sticks for prosperity and arrange them inside of a pretty container. Peruse that listing of common backyard plants for prosperity and work a few plants into your magick. Use the listed components from the other abundance and prosperity spells in this chapter and make some copies of the worksheet! (That's what it's there for.) Try and remember to look to nature first for your prosperity magick supplies. Then create your own enchantments and spells, personalized just for your hearth and home.

Chapter Nine

> *Oh, the fun of arriving at a house*
> *and feeling the spark that tells you*
> *that you are going to have a good time.*
> MARK HAMPTON

HAPPINESS AND HARMONY IN THE HOME

Creating a sense of happiness and harmony in the magickal home has a lot to do with how well you can combine several other magickal aspects in your home. These aspects include a sense of welcome, the overall atmosphere or ambiance of the home, the health and prosperity of the people who live there, and the measure of safety and security that you feel once you are inside.

Wow, that's quite a tall order, isn't it? Well, there is a reason I placed this chapter last, you know. At this point in the game, I wanted you to be able to keep building on all of the information that I have presented so far. Think of all the new ideas you have come up with and the fresh perspectives you've gained on your magickal home. By now you've probably blessed and consecrated the heart of your home and done a little warding work for your thresholds. Did you check out your spice rack to see what you have available for kitchen cupboard conjuring? How did your altar and hearthstone setup turn out? I bet that your outdoor rooms and house plants are happily perking right along. We have covered a lot of magickal topics and taken a look at just about every aspect of natural, hearth, and home magick that I could think of.

So what do we do next? We take all of this magickal information and move it another step further: let's tackle the enchanting topic of creating happiness and harmony within your home.

> *Learn the craft of knowing how to open your heart*
> *and to turn on your creativity.*
> *There's a light inside of you.*
>
> JUDITH JAMISON

HAPPINESS AND HARMONY SPELLS WITH PERSONALITY

The following elemental magick was crafted with you in mind. The supplies are basic, inexpensive, and easy to obtain. As before, check out an arts and crafts store for some of the supplies and try and gather the rest from nature. Take only the smallest amount of natural materials that you'll need. Be a courteous gatherer. Check your own backyard first and see what sort of magickal accessories are available to you. If you are gathering natural materials from someone else's property, always get permission first.

Once again, I encourage you to be creative with the information that is presented in this chapter. A Witch that is generous, practical, and creative makes for one hell of a powerful magickal combination. With this topic, more than ever, it is so important to follow your heart. Go where yours leads you and see what wonders you can achieve as you craft a harmonious and happy home.

AIR MAGICK

Do you feel the need to clear the air? Everybody has squabbles and petty arguments occasionally. My husband and I have been married for over twenty years and we manage to get into tiffs from time to time. Today being no exception. Over what, you are wondering? Car repair, again. I am a "call the mechanic right now" kind of gal. He, on the other hand, likes to putter around and see if he can fix it himself. If not, he takes his time, the mechanic is a friend, and eventually the car gets taken down to the service station.

We bickered and argued over the car until we both realized just how dumb the argument was in the first place. I sat on the living room couch laughing at the irony of writing a chapter on harmony in the home while in the midst of a really stupid argument. Which got me to thinking . . . so I whipped out a notebook and wrote the following spell. This spell is for restoring communication and for clearing the air. I wrote the charm out, sprinkled some lavender inside of the paper, and then folded it up and sealed the note with red sealing wax. I then nonchalantly handed the folded note to my husband and asked him if he thought this spell would work.

He opened it up, trying to dodge the lavender that dumped in his lap, and chuckled at one of my more creative ways of saying "I'm sorry." Here is the charm I wrote that works on restoring communication and harmony in the home (and yes indeed, it worked out just fine).

CLEARING THE AIR SPELL
FOR RESTORING COMMUNICATION

For this spell you will need:

* A piece of paper and a pen (communication symbols)

* A pinch of dried or fresh lavender (lavender is used to de-stress situations, is a cleansing herb, and it is aligned with the element of air)

* Sealing wax and an embosser (optional: you could seal the note with tape)

Write out the charm in your own handwriting. The fold it into thirds. Open the paper back up and sprinkle in a bit of lavender. Next fold the sides up so the lavender stays contained. Then seal the note with sealing wax or a piece of tape. Now give the note to the other person, with an apology. Here is the charm:

Lavender aligns with the element of air,

Restore communication, peace, and love so fair.

Let's clear the air and start this day over brand-new,

Between the two of us, there's nothing we can't do.

FIRE MAGICK

For this fire spell you get to break out several red candles. This spell is designed to bring a little warmth and affection back to a relationship and can be worked on any day. This is for those times when you both seem so caught up in the day-to-day demands that intimacy seems like a far-off dream. Many of us tend to overlook those simple things and sweet, romantic gestures that mean so much. This spell you cast on yourself, to help encourage your own sense of romance, sensuality, and generosity.

FLAMES OF LOVE SPELL

To work this spell, you'll need four red candles and coordinating candleholders. Add a dash of cinnamon to each of the unlit candles, to stir up some more fire energy and to add some more passion. Arrange the work area however you'd like. What natural items do you imagine would add a little spice to this spell and would work best for you? You could try rose petals, or even cinnamon sticks. How about tumbled stones that are associated with the element of fire? Choose from red jasper, garnet, red agate, carnelian, and low-grade rubies. (I found a tumbled ruby for a couple of dollars.)

You could even use red heart-shaped confetti sprinkled around the candles, or scatter a few red glass marbles around the candles to decorate your work area. It's important to get creative and add a little personal flair to this enchantment. If your idea of flair includes special lingerie (I suggest red), then go for it! Once you're all set up, light the candles and repeat the following charm:

See the candle flames flicker and dance so high,

Bring affection softly, like a lover's sigh.

Cherish the qualities that brought us together,

Our love holds true, in both calm and stormy weather.

I now create passion, love, and harmony,

By all the loving power of three times three.

Take a few of the components from the spell, like the crystals or flower petals, and tuck them underneath the mattress of your bed. Allow the candles to burn until they are consumed. I imagine you can figure out what to do next.

WATER MAGICK

These next two watery spells coordinate together. You can either work them separately or simultaneously to help ease tensions and to promote harmony in the home. Try working this spell on a Friday, a Venus day, for extra loving vibrations.

FIRE ON THE WATER SPELL

For the first part of the spell, you will need the following:

* A clear glass bowl

* Water to fill the bowl

* A red floating candle (heart shaped or flower shaped, if possible)

* Essential rose oil (a drop or two)—if that is unavailable, try a drop of vanilla extract (no kidding, it also promotes love)

* A lighter or matches

* A safe, flat surface to set up on

Fill the bowl with water about an inch from the top. Add a drop or two of essential rose oil or the vanilla extract to the water and stir it up in a clockwise motion. Next, send the candle floating across the scented water. Take a moment and visualize peace, loving feelings, and harmony returning to your home. Now light the floating candle and repeat this little charm three times:

> As the candle floats on the water so clear,
> Release all anger and send harmony near.

Allow the floating candle to burn until it goes out on its own. Then take the scented water and sprinkle just a bit of it around the house to reenforce those harmonious vibrations.

The second part of this spell has a rosy magickal project for you. The rose actually corresponds with the element of water, so it's ideal for creating and then enchanting a harmony charm or talisman. Once it's finished, you can hang this talisman up in whatever room you wish—the kitchen, living room, or on your bedroom door.

HEARTS AND ROSES HARMONY CHARM

For this project you will need:

* A dozen silk or dried red rosebuds

* A hot glue gun and glue sticks

* One yard of red or pink quarter-inch-wide satin ribbon

* Essential rose oil and a dropper

Hot glue the rosebuds together into the shape of a heart. Loop twelve inches of the ribbon around the top of the heart to make a hanger. Once the glue sets, take the dropper and drop three drops of rose oil onto the arrangement of flowers. (Don't go overboard with the oil; if you do, the scent will be too strong.) Allow the oil to seep into the flowers. Carefully lift up the arrangement and charge it full of your intentions for creating harmony and peace in your home. Then enchant the heart-shaped talisman with this verse:

Harmony does come from roses shaped like a heart,

Bound up with ribbons and sealed with a Witch's art.

Banish all bad vibes, restore our tranquility,

By all the powers of earth, wind, fire, and sea.

Take the remaining ribbon and fashion a bow; add it to the hanger. As you tie the bow, announce that "the spell is sealed." Hang up the talisman in your chosen spot.

EARTH MAGICK

The graceful, blooming magnolia corresponds to the element of earth. According to flower folklore, planting a magnolia close to your bedroom window ensures a faithful partner. In the language of flowers the magnolia symbolizes a love of nature and encourages determination. The magnolia assures us that better days are just around the corner. This is just the ticket for an earthy spell to increase positive and harmonious vibrations in the home.

For this spell you can either plant the tree on your property or work with the foliage or blossom in your magick. If you want to plant the tree, then head to the nearest garden center or nursery and pick out a young, healthy magnolia to plant into your yard.

If this isn't possible for you, then go on a hunt and see if you have magnolia trees growing locally in the neighborhood. Gather a leaf or two. If you are working the spell in the springtime, then pluck a single blossom from the tree. No luck? Check with a florist for fresh magnolia leaves or try the dried flower section in the arts and crafts store. There are also magnolia-scented candles available.

A TREE BLESSING CHARM FOR HAPPY HOMES

This charm will work for any tree that you plant on your property; just adjust the opening line accordingly. The best time to plant a tree is in the waning moon phase. Once the tree is planted, enchant the tree for healthy growth and to encourage it to add its magick to your home—and don't forget to keep watering it!

The magnolia brings fortitude and fidelity,

Little tree, send happiness and harmony to me.

Grow strong, straight, and true where you now stand,

Your magick spreads out across my land.

MAGNOLIA AND ROSE QUARTZ SPELL FOR HEALTH AND HAPPINESS

Now, for those of you who are unable to plant a magnolia tree, here is an earthy healing spell using a couple of rose quartz tumbled stones and the foliage or blossom of a magnolia tree. If you would like to work a little aromatherapy with this spell, find a few magnolia-scented candles. Typically these are white- to cream-colored, so they can be considered all-purpose.

The scent of magnolia encourages healing, which can come in pretty handy since it's sort of hard to be happy when you're miserable with a cold. This spell is a good one to clear away the blahs and to help you regain your energy when you have a cold or the flu. The best days of the week to work this spell would be a Sunday for sunshiny energy and fitness or a Thursday to tap into Jupiter's energies of healing.

Supplies:

* Two magnolia-scented candles

* Two coordinating candleholders

* Two rose quartz tumbled stones

* Magnolia leaves or a blossom

* A lighter or matches

Arrange your two magnolia candles side by side on your altar or hearthstone setup. Position the foliage and the stones around the candles in a way that pleases you—just make sure to keep any foliage clear of the flames. Light the candles and then repeat the following charm three times:

> *Magnolia has a charming scent, healing it does impart,*
> *Now spin a spell with wisdom from the magick of the hearth.*
> *I call earth for stability, for strength and health that shines,*
> *Send both healing and contentment, let harmony be mine.*

Allow the candles to burn out. Set the stones in a place where you will see them every day, or tuck them into your pocket to reinforce those happy and healthy feelings. You can keep a magnolia leaf or petal with you for a few days, until you start to get back on your feet. Then return the foliage neatly to nature.

An animal's eyes have the power

to speak a great language.

MARTIN BUBER

DOGS AND MAGICK

There is nothing like a faithful pet to welcome you home after a tough day. Pets add so much to our lives. They become part of the family and trusted companions and confidants. Take the dog, for example; the dog is a faithful protector and a friend. There's something about a dog, no matter what breed they are. They can be regal and gorgeous, clever and energetic, or just big and goofy.

I will admit to a love for dogs, but I have a small problem: I'm terribly allergic to them. Every time I pet a dog too much, I break out in big nasty hives, and then I start to sneeze loudly, followed by wheezing. It's really attractive, let me tell you. I get along well enough with dogs, if they are content with a cautious pat or two on the head from me. I envy people who have great relationships with their dogs, as for me this was never a possibility. However, for those of you who share your lives and homes with a canine, here is some magickal lore and tips.

There are a few goddesses associated with the dog, such as Artemis/Diana; the wolfhound, in particular, is associated with her. The Crone goddess, Hecate, is connected with black dogs. Dogs especially sense when Hecate is near; they bark and howl.

Dogs may sense a ghost or warn you of negative influences. If you notice your dog growling at corners and can't place the cause, then I would definitely do a cleansing. Keep the animal with you while you do the cleansing and see if they act differently when you're finished.

If you'd like to work magick for your pet, try enchanting their collars with a little color magick. Purchase a new collar for whatever specific color magick you require. A black or red collar could be enchanted for protection. Try a soft pink collar for your female dog if she is expecting puppies; this should help promote good mother energy for her. A blue or green collar would work out nicely for healing, if your dog had surgery or is ill. You could go with a purple collar to help boost a spiritual connection with your pet, especially if you'd like them to be your familiar. Also, you could paint a star on the back of their ID tags. My friend Nicole hangs a small hematite ring from her dogs' collars, along with their identification tags, to boost her dogs' protection. I'll bet you can come up with even more ideas.

See how your dog reacts to the atmosphere in the home after you perform a cleansing or a blessing. Does your dog stick by your side whenever you cast any spells? Animals are typically sensitive to magickal energy. Do they walk through cast circles or do they sit attentively outside of them? It would be interesting to keep track and see how they react to the magick in your house. You never know, they may have a few new tricks to teach you.

At this point, I am sending your dog a mental scratch behind the ears. I wish both you and your canine friend a long and wonderful life together. Now, here is that pet collar spell for you to try out. Go ahead and adapt and change the words around in the second line to suit your specific magickal purpose, and don't forget to have fun.

I call on Artemis/Diana and Hecate,

Send healing to my pet in the best possible way.

This collar represents the magick of hearth and home,

Always you'll come back to us, no matter where you roam.

Slip the collar onto the dog and close the spell with this line:

For the good of all, with harm to none,

By the hearth and home, this spell is done.

Black cat, cross my path,

good fortune bring to home and hearth . . .

CLAIRE NAHMAD

HOUSE CATS AND MAGICK

Whenever a cat comes into your life, look for magick and mystery to follow. The domestic cat makes a wonderful companion and housemate. An age-old symbol for witchcraft and magick, the cat can add to the energy of your spellcasting and to the overall atmosphere of the home. They are also good barometers of the household energy. A cat that is snoozing the afternoon away in a chair may symbolize peace and contentment. A cat that flies through the house looking for a rumble can be a sign of building negative energies or unhappy vibrations. A cat that leaps and plays by itself is thought to be playing with the faeries.

Adding a few strands of loose cat hair to a hearth and home spell is thought to increase the power of the enchantment. The next time you pet or brush your cat, pick up a couple of those loose hairs. Add them to charm bags or tuck them under a candle for a touch of cat magick. When a circle has been cast, cats seem to like to walk back and forth through the area. I wonder if it gives them a tingle? However, anyone who has a cat knows they have their own set of rules. They either are interested in magick or they're not. That may change tomorrow, never, or maybe in the next moment.

My old orange tabby, Skippy, would always sit at attention on the outside of my circles until I formally invited her in. Then she would flip her tail up high and stroll in to sit at the center of the circle. She wouldn't budge until I was finished. Skippy was definitely my familiar. She usually showed up whenever I was studying magick. She loved to rub her face all over the books, and Skippy always popped up whenever I was casting any spells or writing charms. I miss her still. Isn't it funny how a pet can keep a hold on your heart for years after they have passed on?

Recently our gray tabby cat, Samantha, graced a circle meeting at my house. Typically she ignores the magickal comings and goings. She may jump in a lap for attention but once the magick starts, she finds a good spot to watch and usually takes a nap. A few weeks ago, during a Sabbat ritual, we were all sitting on the living room floor, hands linked, raising energy together. Samantha walked around the circle, purring and rubbing her face on everyone's joined hands, which was quite a surprise.

Around the circle she went, from person to person, causing lots of chuckles from the ladies. Once Samantha had worked her way around the group, she positioned herself regally in the center and sat as still as a statue until we were finished. Will she join us again? With a cat, you never know. They are as unpredictable as the weather.

Which reminds me, did you know that cats are thought to be weather predictors, according to folklore? If your cat sleeps with its head upside down, that means a big change in the weather is forthcoming. There is that old country saying that states, "The cat's sleeping on its brain, it's surely going to rain." That always seems to hold true with my cats. Another way to predict rain was if your cat rolls over on her back, swings her tail playfully at you, and darts her eyes back and forth—supposedly she is communicating with the water spirits and a shower will come soon.

If you have dreams that feature cats, the color of the dream cat has a specific lucky meaning. If you dream of black cats, this symbolizes all-around good luck. The Egyptian cat goddess Bast was typically portrayed as a black cat. Later, the Greco-Roman culture identified Bast with Artemis/Diana. During the Middle Ages, the goddess Diana was called the "Queen of the Witches." Therefore the cat became linked with the Craft and with goddess worship. However, the many different shades and patterns of cats also have folklore and magickal significance attached to them as well.

A tortoiseshell cat signifies that you'll be lucky in love and all manners of the heart. Dreaming of an orange cat is a sure sign of good fortune in business and an increase of your prosperity. Dreams of a black and white cat mean that you are genuinely fond of children and that conception shouldn't be an issue for you. A tabby cat in any color was thought to be a favorite pet among Witches. The striped cat is also a symbol of a happy hearth and home for your family.

Should a smoky gray cat make an appearance in your dreams, they are thought to lead you to hidden treasures. Gray cats are also sacred to the Norse goddess Freya. If gray cats are slinking through your thoughts, perhaps this is Freya's none-too-subtle way of trying to get your attention. Now, a calico cat in a dream symbolizes a close bond with your friends, both old and new. Here's something else to consider about the magickal calico cat: the three traditional calico colors—reddish-orange, white, and black—are triple goddess colors. Finally, if a white cat haunts your dreams, then you'll be blessed with inspiration, foresight, and imagination, and you are an adept at the Craft.

Should you care to try and see a cat in your dreams tonight, then try this charm that calls on the cat goddess Bast and see what wisdom she and her feline messengers may be waiting to impart. Say this charm as you turn in for the night:

> *Goddess Bast, bless me with visions in my dreams this night,*
>
> *Cats are lucky omens, whether black, orange, or white.*
>
> *Softly now, on padded feet you glide into my dreams,*
>
> *Tabby stripes or calico, you are more than you seem.*
>
> *By all the power of three times three,*
>
> *Send your messages gently to me.*

Make happy those who are near,

and those who are far will come.

PROVERB

BACKYARD MAGICK

For our last backyard magick section, let's talk about the maple tree. The maple tree does not usually spring immediately to mind when folks start thinking about magickal trees, probably because it's so common. I imagine most practitioners would choose the rowan or the hawthorn, but oddly enough, those are fairly common as well. Even though this book focuses on the hearth and home, the techniques are all based upon the practice of natural magick. And where do you find those natural magick supplies? You guessed it. You find them outdoors, in nature. So go and take a stroll outside for a moment. Walk around your yard or the neighborhood and really look at those trees. Go find a healthy maple and ask if it's okay if you gently harvest a few leaves. Thank the tree for its help and then make your way back home. We've got some spellcasting to do.

The maple tree is associated with the element of air. Its planetary association is Jupiter. Maple branches may be used to create wands, and the leaves are worked into homey spells and charms designed to bring love, happiness, and prosperity. As the three- to five-lobed leaves turn in the fall, use the various colors of red, orange, and yellow in color magick. Basically, the maple leaf "sweetens spells up." To reinforce the happy vibrations in your home, try working with the foliage of this wonderfully common and enchanting tree.

A MAPLE LEAF SPELL FOR HAPPINESS

Take the maple leaves outside on your deck, patio, or in the backyard on a nice breezy day. Since the element of air is associated with the maple, let's link all this natural magick together. Hold the leaves in the palms of your hands and charge them with your intentions. When a breeze comes along, open your hands and allow the leaves to scatter in the wind. Then say the following verse:

> *I scatter the maple leaves to the four winds,*
> *Bring harmony to my home that never ends.*
> *Send happiness to us by the powers of air,*
> *Bless my home, hearth, and family, with love to spare.*

Allow the leaves to stay where they are, take a deep breath, and turn to face the breeze. While you're out there, ask the element of air to cleanse you of any sadness or negativity you may be holding on to. When you feel finished, sink to the ground for a moment and center yourself. Now stand up, brush off your hands, and go about the rest of your day with a smile.

YARROW, THE WISE WOMAN'S FLOWERING HERB

The yarrow is traditionally associated with wise women, cunning men, and the Craft. This all-purpose flowering herb is a favorite of mine. A perennial, it is easy to grow in sunny, cottage-style gardens. It dries beautifully and is a great magickal flowering herb to have on hand for all sorts of cottage witchery arts and crafts projects, spells, and charms.

The planetary influence for yarrow is Venus, and it is aligned with the element of water. However, its uses are so vast and varied that even if you aren't able to grow your own plants, I would pick up some dried yarrow at an herb shop, magick shop, or at the arts and crafts store to have on hand. Some of yarrow's many uses include promoting harmony between a married couple, encouraging love, increasing psychic abilities, and protection.

If you are looking for a cottage-witchery-style project for your home, or one that makes a great gift for a handfasting or to bless a friend's new home, I've got one for you.

AN ENCHANTED HERBAL BROOM
FOR HEARTH AND HOME
Supplies:

* A small or large decorative broom

* Dried or fresh yellow yarrow (several stems)

* A sprig or two of rosemary (promotes love and good memories)

* Three yards of coordinating ribbons for color magick, or to match the room's décor

* Hot glue gun and sticks

* 22-gauge florist wire or pipe cleaners

* Various charms, ribbons, or a star garland—whatever you can conjure up to make the broom look magickal

Cluster together a little arrangement of the yarrow and the rosemary. Wire them securely together. Now wire the little herbal posy onto the base of the broom handle so that the flowers and foliage rest on the straws or sticks of the broom. (You may wish to glue them down if you're worried about them moving around on you.) Hide the wires with decorative ribbons tied into a bow or wrapped criss-cross style up to the top of the broom's handle. Secure the ribbon with hot glue, if necessary.

Embellish the broom with charms tied onto the ribbons, a decorative bow, or even a glittery star garland if you prefer. Once you have your broom decorated to your liking, enchant it to bring love, harmony, and happiness into the home with the following verse. When you are finished, you can give the broom as a gift or hang it up in a place of honor by your fireplace or hearthstone.

> A *clever Witch's spell I make for happiness and love,*
>
> *This broom sweeps away all sadness from below and above.*
>
> *Yarrow does bring affection, rosemary for memories,*
>
> *A blessing for your hearth and home, and bound by three times three.*

This broom may be used as a symbolic tool or you could use it to sweep any negativity lingering in the home right out of the door.

He is happiest, be he king or peasant,

who finds peace in his home.

JOHANN WOLFGANG VON GOETHE

BIBS, BOBS, AND WHATNOTS

There are all sorts of accessories and whatnots around your home that may be used to promote harmony and happiness. Take a new look around your home with a Witch's eyes and see what you can find.

Take, for example, the bathroom; what do you think you could possibly find in there? Well, you can work healing rituals in the bathtub. Fill up that tub with comfortably hot water and toss in a tablespoon of sea salt, dried lavender, or bubble bath. Light some scented candles and lock the door. Allow yourself to be refreshed and restored by the healing powers of water.

THE CAPTIVATING COMMODE SPELL

One of the funniest things I've ever heard of was using toilet paper in a spell. Write down the problem or name of the person who is causing the problem on the paper, and then flush it down the toilet. It makes you laugh and it helps break the anger or hurt feelings you are carrying around.

Give it a try—fetch some toilet paper from the bathroom. Get a pen and carefully write your problem down on the paper. Then drop it in the toilet bowl and try this silly charm as you flush. There is something so ridiculous and satisfying about watching that paper get sucked down the toilet. If you can do it with a straight face, I'll be very surprised—remember that sometimes laughter is the strongest magick anyone could ever hope to tap into!

I cannot believe that I worried this much,
You're out of my life with the sound of this flush.

Now that we've had a good chuckle, let's think about more magickal accessories found around the house.

FRUIT BOWL BLESSING

For this spell we are heading back to the kitchen. The supplies are simple for this blessing: you'll need a large bowl and some fresh fruit. The fruit itself does have magickal significance, so choose your items carefully. What you want to do is choose a fruit for each magickal quality that you'd like to bring in to your home. Here is a Witch's dozen of easy-to-find magickal fruits. Oh, and here's food for thought . . . you could try adding some of the magickally associated fresh fruit into other spells and charms that were listed throughout this book.

APPLE: wisdom and prophecy

BANANA: fertility and passion (well, just think about it . . .)

BLUEBERRY: psychic protection

CHERRY: love

GRAPES: prosperity and fertility

LEMON: cleansing, hex-breaking

LIME: promotes good health and security

ORANGE: healing and sunshine

PEAR: lust and love, also justice

PLUM: fruitfulness and abundance

POMEGRANATE: wishes granted, fertility, protection

RASPBERRY: fertility and pregnancy

STRAWBERRY: passion, motherhood, and safe pregnancy

Arrange the chosen fruit into the bowl and then place a white all-purpose candle off to the side. (A little tealight in a holder would be ideal for this spell.) Enchant the fruit, so all of the various magickal properties go swirling out into your home and happily into the folks who snack on them. After you're done working this spell, eat some of the fruit yourself.

To work this spell, light the candle and then hold your hands over the fresh fruit. Empower the fruit bowl with the following charm:

I bless this fresh fruit for health and for a loving spell,

Grant your powers to my family that's loved so well.

This candle stands for the homey charm I have spun,

For the happiness of all, and let it harm none.

Allow the candle to burn out. Leave the fruit on the counter or table for healthy snacks.

A picture is worth a thousand words.

FAMILIAR SAYING

PRACTICAL FAMILY PHOTOGRAPH MAGICK

Family photos are good props to work with. You can encircle them with salt to break negativity, or a photo can be tucked under a candleholder to help focus the spell on the individual—this would be a great link in a healing spell. Having a squabble with a relative? Try placing their photo inside of a shallow bowl and cover the picture with sugar to help end hard feelings and to allow peace and healing to begin. If a picture is worth a thousand words, there must be at least a thousand or so ways to work affirmative magick with a photograph.

In a few of the spells in this book, photos were used as props. Experiment with this for yourself; see what sort of personalized magick you can create. Yeah, I'm being tough this time. Now is when you get to write your own charms. Take a look at chapter 3 and chapter 8—there are two spell worksheets there for you. Make copies and start working on your own witchy ideas for hearth and home. You can do it. Making magick individual and working in your own personality and style is what makes spellcasting powerful.

Shut the door, not that it lets in the cold
but that it lets out the coziness.

MARK TWAIN

CLOSING THOUGHTS

As we close up this cozy book on the natural magick of hearth and home, I hope that you've enjoyed yourself. I am so glad that you decided to spend some time with me. Now that you've worked your way through this book of cottage witchery, I'll bet that you will never look at your home the same way again. As we've come to see, magick is everywhere.

It requires heart and determination to create a better life and home for yourself and your loved ones. Take the ideas and spells that were presented here and make them uniquely your own. Get to know the deities of the hearth; start to work with the house faeries. Create your own little hearthstone setup and ask for the blessings of the goddesses Brigid, Vesta, and Hestia. They are waiting for you—call on them and see what you discover.

Take a look at the household journal that is provided in the back of this book. There are even more spells and charms tucked in there for you. This is the perfect opportunity to personalize the various magick that is included in this book. You could easily use this journal space as your own private magickal notebook for hearth and home. Go ahead, list the spices you have in your kitchen cupboard and start plotting how you will incorporate them into homemade enchantments. Experiment and work with the energy of the four elements to improve the quality of your life and the atmosphere of wherever you call home.

Cottage witchery is my way of encouraging you to bring both the beauty and the charm of nature into your home with simple enchantments and down-to-earth magick. Now add all these new witchy skills that you've learned to your magickal repertoire every day, in both simple and profound ways. They are sure to bring a natural wonder to your life.

Remember: home is where the heart is, as they say. I have always maintained that the strongest and truest magick does indeed come from the heart.

From my hearth to yours, this homey magick was spun,

Trust in your own power and the charm is begun.

Look inside yourself, for the true magick is there,

All you have to do is to know, to will, and to dare.

KITCHEN CUPBOARD CONJURING
MAGICKAL SPICE & HERB LIST

Spice: _____ Magickal Use: _____

Spice: _____ Magickal Use: _____

Spice: _____ Magickal Use: _____

Spice: _____ Magickal Use: _____

Spice: _____ Magickal Use: _____

Spice: _____ Magickal Use: _____

Spice: _____ Magickal Use: _____

Spice: _____ Magickal Use: _____

Spice: _____ Magickal Use: _____

Spice: _____ Magickal Use: _____

Spice: _____ Magickal Use: _____

Spice: _____ Magickal Use: _____

Spice: _____ Magickal Use: _____

Spice: _____ Magickal Use: _____

Variety's the very spice of life.

WILLIAM COWPER

Dried and crumbled betony (perennial lamb's ears) sprinkled around the perimeter of your home creates a protective boundary and promotes security.

_____

_____

_____

_____

_____

> *If you want a golden rule that will*
> *fit everybody, this is it:*
> *Have nothing in your houses that you do not know*
> *to be useful, or believe to be beautiful.*
>
> **WILLIAM MORRIS**

_____

_____

_____

_____

_____

_____

_____

_____

_____

_____

_____

_____

_____

_____

> May I a small house and large garden have;
> And a few friends, and many books true,
> Both wise, and both delightful too!

ABRAHAM CROWLEY

Feeling exhausted after work? Try adding a few drops of sweet orange oil to an unscented tealight. Burn the candle in whatever room you are in and relax for a few moments. Repeat this charm:

> By the power of scent and candlelight,
> Please help me catch my second wind tonight.

* * *

To find a missing household item, or even a pet, visualize it circled with a silver rope. Now imagine gathering the rope and the item back to you. Say:

> What was lost now is found,
> As my magick circles 'round.

_____

_____

_____

_____

_____

_____

_____

_____

_____

_____

_____

_____

_____

_____

_____

_____

_____

_____

To counteract household faery mischief, leave a few quartz crystal points on the hearth overnight. The faeries enjoy shiny objects and this will encourage them to leave your car keys alone.

> *No house should ever be on a hill or on anything.*
> *It should be of the hill, belonging to it,*
> *so hill and house could live together*
> *each the happier for the other.*
>
> FRANK LLOYD WRIGHT

To enchant a household broom for magickal purposes, sprinkle the bristles with a few drops of water and a pinch of salt, and fan some incense smoke over the broom. Then place both hands on the broom and say:

> *The proper Witch's broom is not used for midnight flights,*
> *Instead, it brushes out harm and sweeps in love and light.*

Now display the broom in a prominent place of honor.

Oh, to have a little house!

To own the hearth and stool and all!

PADRAIC COLUM

A *new broom sweeps clean.*

FAMILIAR SAYING

BROOMSTICK SPELL 1: REMOVING GLOOM

Here is a quick spell that can be performed with a household or a ritual broom. First, sweep the room clean and visualize all negativity being brushed right out the door. Work in a banishing (counterclockwise) direction. As you finish sweeping the dust and dirt out of your home, close the spell with this line:

All negativity must leave this room,

As I sweep away all the dust and gloom!

Happy is the house that shelters a friend.

RALPH WALDO EMERSON

BROOMSTICK SPELL 2:
SWEEPING AWAY BAD LUCK
FROM THE THRESHOLD

Sweep your home clean from top to bottom. Leave a little pile of dust and dirt close to the front door; dispose of the rest. Now go to that last remaining pile of dirt and open the door. Take a deep breath and visualize your front door surrounded by a blue, glowing light. Now sweep the remainder of the dirt out the door and over your threshold, and off your front porch or steps. As you do this, repeat the charm quietly three times:

As I sweep away bad luck with this enchanted broom,
Negativity must flee to the sound of this tune.
This threshold is protected and surrounded with light,
My home is warded and secure both day and night.

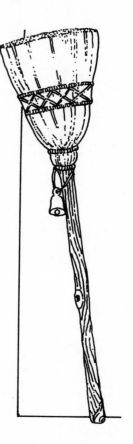

_____

_____

_____

_____

_____

Who shall say I am not the

happy genius of my household?

WILLIAM CARLOS WILLIAMS

❧

_____

_____

_____

_____

_____

_____

_____

_____

_____

_____

_____

Arrange apples, ornamental corn, and miniature pumpkins in a basket.
Set these on your kitchen table and enchant them for
wisdom, prosperity, and a happy harvest season.

BANISHING GHOSTS AND THINGS
THAT GO "BUMP" IN THE NIGHT

Do you think you have a ghost or bad energy hanging around? If possible, work this spell in a waning moon phase to tie into the banishing energies of the moon. Alternatively, try a Saturday (Saturn's day) to remove the problem and to pull in the closing energies of the week.

Take two bristles from your ritual or household broom and burn them inside of a cauldron or old pot. Next sprinkle all of the inside corners of the house with salt, blessed water, and incense smoke. Go to the center of the house and announce:

In the name of the Lady, and by the power of a Witch's art,

All spells and energies not in harmony with me must now depart!

Finally, take the blessed water and draw small stars on every door, window, and mirror. (This seals up the house so nothing else, like sour vibes or negativity, can get in.) Once the water dries, the stars will be invisible but the magick will remain.

Got the writing bug? Put a carnelian, tiger's-eye, and malachite stone by your writing desk. They encourage eloquence, energy, and business success.

An idea can turn to dust or magic, depending on the talent that rubs against it.

WILLIAM BERNBACH

MAGICKAL LIBRARY PROTECTION CHARM

This charm calls on Sheshat, the Egyptian goddess whose title was "Mistress of the House of Books." Fan a bit of your favorite incense smoke over your books and bookshelves at home and repeat the following charm three times:

> *Sheshat, Mistress of the House of Books, hear my call,*
>
> *Guard and protect these magickal tomes, one and all.*
>
> *If borrowed, may the book always return safely to me,*
>
> *I bind this charm with the powers of earth, air, flame, and sea.*

* * *

BEDROOM BLESSING

Work this enchantment on the night of a full moon. Incorporate a little something from each of the four elements for this blessing and have fun.

> *Goddess, bless this bedroom where we sleep, love, and dream,*
>
> *By the light of the moon things are not as they seem.*
>
> *A pinch of salt for earth, a sprinkle of water for love,*
>
> *Candlelight brings passion, a breeze sends insight from above.*
>
> *Elements four circle merrily around this boudoir,*
>
> *As I cast enchantment to the corners, both near and far.*

_____
_____
_____
_____
_____
_____
_____
_____
_____
_____
_____
_____
_____
_____
_____
_____

Set out a few clusters of quartz crystals in the heart of your home.
It keeps the family on a positive track.

Children's Bedroom Blessing

Goddess, bless this bedroom where my children play, sleep, and dream,

For a child's imagination is a wonderful thing.

Now add a touch of faery dust and a houseful of love,

As I conjure joy and receive your blessings from above.

Paint a baby's room in soft blue or pale green to promote
a calming atmosphere and a healthy environment.

If you are hoping to conceive a child, try putting yellow sheets on the bed.
The color is supposed to encourage creativity.

_____

_____

_____

_____

_____

_____

_____

_____

_____

_____

A sprig of rosemary beneath your pillow promotes restful sleep and untroubled dreams.
Tuck the rosemary underneath and say:

This magick rosemary that smells so sweet

Sends to me pleasant dreams and peaceful sleep.

To clear out any negativity in the house, open the windows for a few moments and ask the element of air to blow away all sour vibes and hurt feelings. Say:

Element of air, on you I call,

Remove the bad vibes from one and all.

Go little book, and wish to all,

Flowers in the garden, meat in the hall,

A bin of wine, a spice of wit,

A house with lawns enclosing it,

A living river by the door,

A nightingale in the sycamore!

ROBERT LOUIS STEVENSON

ANNUAL: A plant that completes its life cycle in one growing season.

ARTEMIS: The Greek goddess of the moon and of the hunt; twin sister to Apollo. A maiden goddess who protected women in childbirth and who was associated with wild animals and the domestic dog.

ASTRAL BEING: A spirit or elemental energy conjured for a specific magickal purpose, such as protection.

ASTRAL PLANE: The plane of existence where magick lives. This plane is just beyond our physical one—it cannot usually be seen, but it can be felt and accessed through magick.

BANISHING: Repelling an unwanted person, situation, or psychic entity.

BAST: The Egyptian cat-headed goddess of love, magick, and fertility.

BRIGID: The Celtic goddess of the hearth flame. A well-loved triple goddess of healing, smithcraft, and poetry. Her festival is a major Sabbat in the Wiccan calendar, February 1, which is known as Brigid's day, Candlemas, or Imbolc.

BROWNIES: A benevolent house faery and an earth elemental. They have many different names from many cultures, such as Bwca and Hobs. (See chapter 4.)

CAULDRON: A large kettle, typically iron, with three legs. A Witch's tool representing the element of water and a goddess symbol of regeneration and rebirth.

CHARGING: To load an object full of your magickal intention. Typically this is done by holding the object and then visualizing your magickal will and energy flowing into it.

CHARM: A rhyming series of words (a spell) used for a specific magickal purpose.

Glossary

COTTAGE WITCHERY: A style of natural magick that revolves around the hearth and magickal home.

COVEN/CIRCLE: A group of Wiccans that worship and study together.

THE CRAFT: The Witch's name for the Old Religion and practice of Witchcraft.

CUNNING MEN: Cunning men were the healers and keepers of the ancient magickal knowledge—the male version of a wise woman. They were the original wise men.

DEOSIL: Moving in a clockwise direction for casting circles, stirring up potions, and bringing forth positive influences.

DIANA: The Roman goddess of the hunt. Diana is a maiden moon goddess and is also associated with dogs. Diana became associated with the Craft in the Middle Ages when she gained the title of "Queen of the Witches." A popular goddess in the Craft today, she represents freedom, women's mysteries, and being daring enough to stand on your own.

DIVINATION: The art and practice that seeks to foresee or foretell future events or hidden knowledge. Divination may be accomplished by means of tarot cards, scrying, tea-leaf reading, or runes.

ELEMENTALS: Spirits or energies that coordinate with each element. Earth elementals are brownies and gnomes; air elementals are faeries and sylphs; water elementals are undines; and fire elementals are salamanders and dragons. (See chapters 4 and 8 for more magickal information on the fire elementals.)

ELEMENTS: Earth, air, fire, and water.

FAERY: A nature spirit. Usually an earth or air elemental.

FENG SHUI: Means literally "wind and water." The 5,000-year-old practice of arranging and decorating your home to promote prosperity and contentment by manipulating chi, or positive energy. (See chapter 2.)

FLOWER FASCINATIONS: The use of flowers in spellwork. A fascination is the art of directing another's consciousness or will toward you to command or to bewitch.

GARDEN WITCH: A practical, down-to-earth type of practitioner. A Witch who is well versed in herbal knowledge and its uses, and who is a magickal gardener.

GREEN MAGICK: The magick of the natural world. Working with the elements, plants, and trees.

GROUNDING AND CENTERING: A visualization technique. A way to focus and relax before and after performing magick. You push away negativity and stress from your own body, then pull back into your body healthy, calm, and strong energy from the earth.

HESTIA: The Greek goddess of the hearth flame. Hestia was an important goddess of her time. Homemaking and family life were especially revered by Hestia. (See chapter 4.)

HEX SIGNS: A wooden disc painted in bright colors that features geometric designs. A type of American folk art, the hex sign brings good luck, prosperity, and protection to the home that it is displayed in or on. (See chapter 1 for more information.)

HOUSE FAERIES: Benevolent faeries and elementals of the hearth and home. (See chapter 4.)

KITCHEN WITCH: A hearth and home practitioner. One who celebrates and practices their Craft in a quiet way using household tools, herbs, and spices.

MAGICK: The combination of your personal power used in harmony with the powers of natural objects such as crystals, herbs, and the elements.

MIDSUMMER: The summer solstice, this typically falls on or around June 21, the longest day of the year and the shortest night. An opportune time to work with the faeries.

NATURAL MAGICIAN: A magician who works their magick mainly with the elements, in harmony with herbs and nature.

PYROMANCY: Divination by gazing into a fire or candleflames. (See chapter 4.)

RULE OF THREE: The Rule of Three states that whatever magick you send out will be returned to you in kind. For the record, the rule of three goes like this: "Ever mind the rule of three, three times what you send out returns to thee."

SALAMANDERS: A fire elemental. (See chapter 4.)

SAMHAIN: Also known as Halloween, this holiday is also a major Sabbat. Samhain begins at sunset on October 31 and is celebrated as the Witches' New Year and the beginning of the Celtic year. This harvest festival is a time to remember your loved ones who have passed on and to be thankful for your blessings.

SCRYING: To scry is to divine the future by gazing into a reflective surface such as water, a dark convex mirror, or a living flame. (See chapter 4.)

TALISMAN: An object similar to an amulet, designed for a specific magickal purpose.

TASSEOGRAPHY: Tea-leaf reading. (See chapter 3.)

TRIPLE MOON GODDESS: Refers to the three faces of the Goddess: the Maiden, who is symbolized by the new crescent moon; the Mother, who is represented by the full moon; and the Crone, who is associated with the waning and dark moon. One example of such a trinity would be Artemis, Selene, and Hecate.

WARDING: Protection magick. A sort of psychic alarm system used to guard your home. (See chapter 1.)

WICCA: The contemporary name for the religion of the Witch. Wicca takes its roots from the Anglo-Saxon word *wicce*, which may mean "wise." Another definition is "to shape or to bend." A Pagan religion based on the cycles of nature and a belief in harming none, karma, reincarnation, and the worship of both a god and a goddess.

WIDDERSHINS: Working in a counterclockwise (banishing) direction.

WISE WOMEN: The first Witches and the custodians of the herbal knowledge of benevolent spells and charms. They were the healers and wise folk of their communities.

WITCHCRAFT: The Craft of the Witch.

WITCHES' REDE: The absolute rule that Witches and magick users live by. The Rede states simply, "An' it harm none, do what ye will."

VESTA: The Roman goddess of the hearth. She was held in a place of honor in the ancient home. The tasks of housekeeping and fire making were sacred to Vesta. Vesta's temple was guarded by her priestesses, the vestal virgins. (See chapter 4.)

YULE: The winter solstice; the shortest day and the longest night of the year. Typically Yule falls on or around December 21. A Wiccan Sabbat that celebrates the return of the newly born Sun god and the Mother Goddess. Gift giving and the familiar symbols of decorated pine trees, wreaths, suns, and lights all have Pagan roots, and are part of our celebration.

YULE LOG: A candle-studded log decorated with holly, ivy, and evergreen. Used in winter solstice celebrations. (See chapter 5.)

To feel most beautifully alive means to be
reading something beautiful, ready always
to apprehend in the flow of language
the sudden flash of poetry.
GASTON BACHELARD

Adams, Anton and Mina Adams. *The Learned Arts of Witches and Wizards.* New York: Barnes and Noble Books, 2000.

Ban Breathnach, Sarah. *Simple Abundance: A Daybook of Comfort and Joy.* New York: Warner Books, 1995.

Brown, Simon. *Practical Feng Shui.* New York: Sterling Publishing Company, 1997.

Borland, Hal. *Plants of Christmas.* New York: Golden Press, 1969.

Budapest, Zsuzsanna. *The Grandmother of Time.* San Francisco: Harper and Row, 1989.

Caringer, Denise L., ed. *Cottage Style.* Des Moines: Better Homes and Gardens Books, 1998.

Conway, D. J. *Moon Magick.* St. Paul: Llewellyn, 1995.

Cook, Jim. *Do You Know What I Know? The Symbols of Christmas.* Self-published, 1997.

Cunningham, Scott and David Harrington. *The Magical Household.* St. Paul: Llewellyn, 1983.

Cunningham, Scott. *Cunningham's Encyclopedia of Magical Herbs.* St Paul: Llewellyn, 1985.

———. *Cunningham's Encyclopedia of Crystal, Gem and Metal Magic.* St. Paul: Llewellyn, 1992.

Dolnick, Barrie. *Simple Spells for Hearth and Home*. New York: Harmony Books, 2000.

Dugan, Ellen. *Garden Witchery: Magick from the Ground Up*. St. Paul: Llewellyn, 2003.

———. *Elements of Witchcraft: Natural Magick for Teens*. St. Paul: Llewellyn, 2003.

———. "Autumn Enchantments." *Llewellyn's 2005 Witches' Datebook*. St. Paul: Llewellyn, 2004.

———. "How to Be a Thoroughly Modern Witch Mom." *Llewellyn's 2003 Wicca Almanac*. St. Paul: Llewellyn, 2002.

———. "Money Magic." *Llewellyn's 2004 Magical Almanac*. St. Paul: Llewellyn, 2003.

———. *7 Days of Magick: Spells, Charms and Correspondences for the Bewitching Week*. St. Paul: Llewellyn, 2004.

Engelbreit, Mary. *Time for Tea!* Kansas City: Andrews McMeel Publishing, 1997.

Gallagher, Anne-Marie. *Magical Spells for Your Home*. Hauppage, NY: Barron's, 2002.

Gilmer, Maureen. *The Gardener's Way: A Daybook of Acts and Affirmations*. Chicago: Contemporary Books, 2001.

Grounds for Gardening. University Extension, University of Missouri-Columbia, 1999. (A Master Gardener reference guide.)

Hallam, Linda, ed. *Garden Style*. Des Moines: Better Homes and Gardens Books, 1999.

Hodson, Geoffrey. *Fairies at Work and at Play*. Wheaton, IL: The Theosophical Publishing House, 1982.

Knight, Sirona. *Faery Magick*. Franklin Lakes, NJ: New Page Books, 2003.

March, Marion D. and Joan McEvers. *The Only Way to Learn Astrology*. Vol. I. San Diego: Astro-Analytic Publications, 1976.

Matthews, John. *The Winter Solstice*. Wheaton, IL: Quest Books, 1998.

Nahmad, Claire. *Cat Spells*. Philadelphia: Running Press, 1993.

Rowinski, Kate, ed. *The Quotable Cook*. New York: Lyons Press, 2000.

Randolph, Vance. *Ozark Magic and Folklore*. New York: Dover Publications, 1964.

RavenWolf, Silver. *Hex Craft: Dutch Country Pow-Wow Magick*. St. Paul: Llewellyn, 1995.

———. *Silver's Spells for Protection*. St. Paul: Llewellyn, 2000.

Rossbach, Sarah. *Interior Design with Feng Shui*. New York: Penguin Putnam, 1991.

Starhawk. *The Spiral Dance*. 10th Anniversary Edition. San Francisco: Harper Collins, 1989.

Telesco, Patricia. *A Kitchen Witch's Cookbook*. St. Paul: Llewellyn, 1994.

———. *A Victorian Grimoire*. St. Paul: Llewellyn, 1993.

Tourtillott, Suzanne. *Decorating Porches and Decks: And Stylish Projects for Outdoor Rooms*. New York: Sterling Publishing, 2001.

Valiente, Doreen. *An ABC of Witchcraft*. Custer, WA: Phoenix Publishing, 1973.

———. *Natural Magic*. Custer, WA: Phoenix Publishing, 1975.

Walker, Barbara G. *The Woman's Dictionary of Sacred Symbols and Objects*. Edison, NJ: Castle Books, 1988.

☽ LLEWELLYN ORDERING INFORMATION

Order Online:
Visit our website at www.llewellyn.com, select your books, and order them on our secure server.

Order by Phone:
- Call toll-free within the U.S. at 1-877-NEW-WRLD (1-877-639-9753). Call toll-free within Canada at 1-866-NEW-WRLD (1-866-639-9753)
- We accept VISA, MasterCard, and American Express

Order by Mail:
Send the full price of your order (MN residents add 7% sales tax) in U.S. funds, plus postage & handling to:
Llewellyn Worldwide
P.O. Box 64383, Dept. 0-7387-0625-6
St. Paul, MN 55164-0383, U.S.A.

Postage & Handling:
Standard (U.S., Mexico, & Canada). If your order is:
Up to $25.00, add $3.50
$25.01 - $48.99, add $4.00
$49.00 and over, FREE STANDARD SHIPPING
(Continental U.S. orders ship UPS. AK, HI, PR, & P.O. Boxes ship USPS 1st class. Mex. & Can. ship PMB.)

International Orders:
Surface Mail: For orders of $20.00 or less, add $5 plus $1 per item ordered. For orders of $20.01 and over, add $6 plus $1 per item ordered.

Air Mail:
Books: Postage & Handling is equal to the total retail price of all books in the order.
Non-book items: Add $5 for each item.

Orders are processed within 2 business days.
Please allow for normal shipping time. Postage and handling rates subject to change.

GARDEN WITCHERY
Magick from the Ground Up
(Includes a Gardening Journal)

Ellen Dugan

HOW DOES YOUR MAGICKAL GARDEN GROW?

Garden Witchery is more than belladonna and wolfsbane. It's about making your own enchanted backyard with the trees, flowers, and plants found growing around you. It's about creating your own flower fascinations and spells, and it's full of common-sense information about cold hardiness zones, soil requirements, and a realistic listing of accessible magickal plants.

There may be other books on magickal gardening, but none have practical gardening advice, magickal correspondences, flower folklore, moon gardening, faery magick, advanced witchcraft, and humorous personal anecdotes all rolled into one volume.

0-7387-0318-4
272 pp., 7.5 x 7.5 $16.95

7 DAYS OF MAGIC
Spells, Charms & Correspondences
for the Bewitching Week

Ellen Dugan

EVERY DAY IS A BEWITCHING DAY

Enchantment is not limited to the Sabbats and the occasional full moon. Magic happens all the time and every day. *7 Days of Magic* demonstrates how to successfully apply the specific magical energies of each day into spells, charms, and rituals.

Forget about memorizing massive correspondence charts. This practical, easy-to-use guide encourages readers to learn at their own pace. Every chapter—one for each day of the week—contains a small table of magical correspondences (planetary influence and symbol, deities, flowers and plants, metals, colors, crystals and stones, Tarot cards, herbs and spices), which are talked about in-depth within seven distinct sections. Each chapter ends with a magickal potpourri of sample spells and rituals.

0-7387-0589-6
240 pp., 7.5 x 7.5

$12.95

🕸 To Write to the Author 🕸

If you wish to contact the author or would like more information about this book, please write to the author in care of Llewellyn Worldwide and we will forward your request. Both the author and publisher appreciate hearing from you and learning of your enjoyment of this book and how it has helped you. Llewellyn Worldwide cannot guarantee that every letter written to the author can be answered, but all will be forwarded. Please write to:

Ellen Dugan
℅ Llewellyn Worldwide
P.O. Box 64383, Dept. 0-7387-0625-6
St. Paul, MN 55164-0383, U.S.A.
Please enclose a self-addressed stamped envelope for reply,
or $1.00 to cover costs. If outside U.S.A., enclose
international postal reply coupon.

Many of Llewellyn's authors have websites with additional information and resources. For more information, please visit our website:

HTTP://WWW.LLEWELLYN.COM